THE WORKBENCH TREASURY OF

Wooden Toy Projects

for the HOME CRAFTSMAN

by the Staff of WORKBENCH Magazine

Modern Handcraft, Inc.
Kansas City

ATTENTION: SCHOOLS AND BUSINESS FIRMS
Modern Handcraft books are available at quantity discounts for bulk
purchases for educational, business or sales promotional use.

All inquiries should be addressed to Modern Handcraft, Inc.
4251 Pennsylvania, Kansas City, Missouri 64111

Printed in the United States of America

Library of Congress Cataloging in Publication Data
The Workbench Treasury of Wooden Toy Projects.

1. Wooden toy making. I. Workbench.
TT174.5.W6W67   745.592   81-83667
ISBN 0-86675-003-7   AACR2

Contents

Introduction 4
Stacking ring clown 5
Pelican pull toy 5
Walking bunny 6
Stacking wagon pull toy 7
Lacing boot bank 8
Tiny tot's rocking horse 9
Toddler rocking horse chair 10
Rocking zebra 11
Two-way tot's teeter/slide 12
Little red barn 14
Miniature wooden toy cars 15
Village blocks 18
Building blocks 20
Gravity marble game 21
Bulldozer 22
Dump truck 23
Motor home 24
Tug and barge 26
Biplane 27
Helicopter 28
Antique "Dolly Madison" coupe 29
Junior steam train 30
Ride'em steam train 32
Ride'em riverboat 35
Prancing pony wheelbarrow 37
Cedar toy chest 38
Circus wagon and toy box 38
Two locomotive toy boxes 40
Boxcar toy box 42
Tank car toy box 43
Caboose toy box 44
Pioneer cradle 46
Doll size bedroom furniture 48
The Borden dollhouse 50
Toddler sled 55
Children's surrey sled 56

Introduction

The wonderful world of wooden toys for little girls and boys offers rewarding opportunities for you as a home craftsman. With the plans in this book as your guide, you can build appreciated and lasting playthings that will be long remembered. You can enjoy hours of hobby-crafting, demonstrate your woodworking expertise, and maybe even satisfy that urge to be creative.

The scope of this book goes far beyond the limits of a mere collection of toy plans. Drawn from nearly a quarter century of the most popular WORKBENCH magazine toy projects, this selection typifies WORKBENCH's rigid criteria for children's playthings.

Above all else, WORKBENCH toys must be CHILD-SAFE. Users of this book are urged not to take shortcuts, nor to substitute unsafe materials that might in any way be potentially dangerous to a child. Sharp edges, slivery or splintery wood, protruding hardware, poisonous lead-based paints, glass, and shatterable plastics are examples of things that are purposely avoided in WORKBENCH toy plans.

Secondly, toys must be FUN for those who will play with them. Each of these projects was actually built by WORKBENCH readers, each has been fun-tested with children.

To qualify for inclusion in this book, each toy had to have the capability of being HOMEMADE in a home craftsman's own workshop. Alternatives to basic plans are suggested in some instances, and creativity by the reader is always encouraged.

ORIGINALITY of design sets these playtime treasures apart from all others. Some of these toys are unique and not found anywhere else. Some are heirloom types to be handed down from generation to generation with only a fresh coat of paint to mark the passing years.

Finally, because child's play is in fact an EDUCATIONAL process, these toys are designed to aid in teaching children wholesome pursuits befitting their tender years.

We have attempted to simplify plans, keep explanations short and to the point, and have translated technical terms into conversational language wherever possible. Please note that in many cases SQUARED DRAWINGS are used, mainly because those particular projects are best dimensioned to fit the size of a particular youngster, or a specific application. To enlarge to actual size from a squared drawing, first determine the scale you need.

That is to say, you determine that one side of an individual square in the original drawing equals one inch, or two inches, or whatever scale you set. Then draw a full size grid of these actual size squares in pen or pencil on paper or on the actual stock to be used. Finally, draw in the details of the toy in the same relative positions in the squares of the full size drawing.

Measuring the child's leg length, arm length, height, or whatever other measurement is appropriate, will aid you in determining what scale to use. Be sure to allow for the fact that children grow rapidly. Squared drawings make it easier to adapt the plans to the actual dimensions of stock you will be using.

Because many of these toys require small, wooden wheels, here is a clever way of sanding them into true round. Attach the rough-cut wheels to axles in a block of wood, or directly to the toy if of appropriate size. Then "drive" the wheels on a belt sander. The motion of the belt will cause the wheels to rotate. Now by turning the wheels at a slight angle to the sanding belt a scuffing action will result that will sand the wheels smooth and make the outside diameters concentric with the axles at the same time.

Best of success in your toymaking efforts!

Stacking Ring Clown

Very often the most simple toy is the best one. This toddler's stacking toy is a case in point. It is simply disks of wood cut from 1-1/4 in. softwood. Each disk has a 3/4 in. hole bored in the center that then is sanded to provide an easy sliding fit on a 3/4 in. dowel.

The several disks, as shown in the drawing, stack on the dowel that is glued into the bottom disk.

The head of the clown is turned on a lathe and sanded smooth. A 3/4 in. blind hole is drilled in the bottom of the head so it will fit over the top of the dowel. Be sure the clown head is not so small it could be swallowed by a child.

Also be sure the enamel you use is nontoxic and safe for children. If you paint the dowel, be sure the holes in the disks still slip easily over the dowel.

Glue a piece of felt or cork to the underside of the bottom disk to protect surfaces on which the clown is placed.

Pelican Pull Toy

Toddlers will be enchanted with this friendly pull toy that "talks" as they pull him along, a simple wire linkage opening and closing his voluminous beak. All parts of the toy can be made from scraps of wood you probably have in your shop.

The base is 3/4 in. plywood or 1 in. solid stock, the body is 1/2 or 3/4 in. material and the wings and beak halves are 1/4 in. stock. Make cardboard patterns of the various pieces from the squared drawings, then saw out the shapes.

If you have no lathe for turning the wheels, first draw them on your stock and saw them out slightly oversize. Bore a hole through the center of each wheel, slip a nut and bolt through the hole and chuck it in a drill press or variable speed drill and "turn" each wheel to size with a rasp, file and sandpaper on a block of wood.

The linkage is formed from coat hanger wire, while the front axle can be slightly heavier wire or a long nail. The rear axles are No. 8 x 1-1/2 in. flathead wood screws countersunk into the wheel.

The only part of the toy that may present problems is the linkage. If the beak does not move freely, move it forward slightly; the brads used will not make large holes and can be tapped in lightly before checking the operation. When the beak works freely, tap them in all the way.

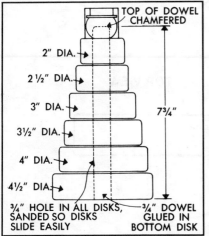

Drawing labels (left diagram):
- TOP OF DOWEL CHAMFERED
- 2" DIA.
- 2½" DIA.
- 3" DIA.
- 3½" DIA.
- 4" DIA.
- 4½" DIA.
- 7¾"
- ¾" HOLE IN ALL DISKS, SANDED SO DISKS SLIDE EASILY
- ¾" DOWEL GLUED IN BOTTOM DISK

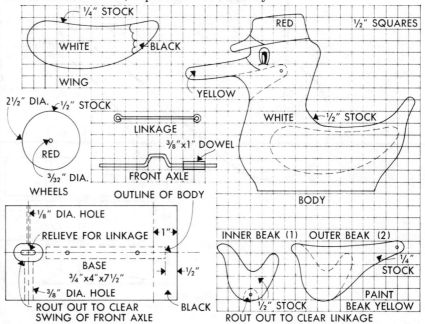

Drawing labels (right diagram):
- ¼" STOCK
- WHITE
- BLACK
- WING
- RED
- ½" SQUARES
- YELLOW
- WHITE
- ½" STOCK
- LINKAGE
- 2½" DIA.
- ½" STOCK
- RED
- 3/32" DIA.
- WHEELS
- 3/8"x1" DOWEL
- FRONT AXLE
- OUTLINE OF BODY
- BODY
- ⅛" DIA. HOLE
- RELIEVE FOR LINKAGE
- 1"
- BASE ¾"x4"x7½"
- ½"
- 3/8" DIA. HOLE
- ROUT OUT TO CLEAR SWING OF FRONT AXLE
- INNER BEAK (1)
- OUTER BEAK (2)
- ¼" STOCK
- ½" STOCK
- PAINT BEAK YELLOW
- BLACK
- ROUT OUT TO CLEAR LINKAGE

Walking Bunny

The lifelike action of this "walking bunny" will captivate both young and old, and it can be built in an hour or so with a few pieces of scrap wood.

Use 1/2 to 3/4 in. wood of close and uniform grain. Uniformity of the wood density and weight is essential for good balance. Cut around the pattern lines with either a jig saw or coping saw, then drill the 3/8 in. holes in the body and legs.

To assemble, glue dowels in one leg, put a washer on the pivoting dowel, add the body and a second washer, rub glue on ends of dowels and push on second leg. Avoid using excess glue. Before glue sets assure proper clearance between legs and body for action.

If you wish to paint the bunny, do so before assembling. Place the bunny on an inclined board and he will walk down it all by himself with a "determined" gait.

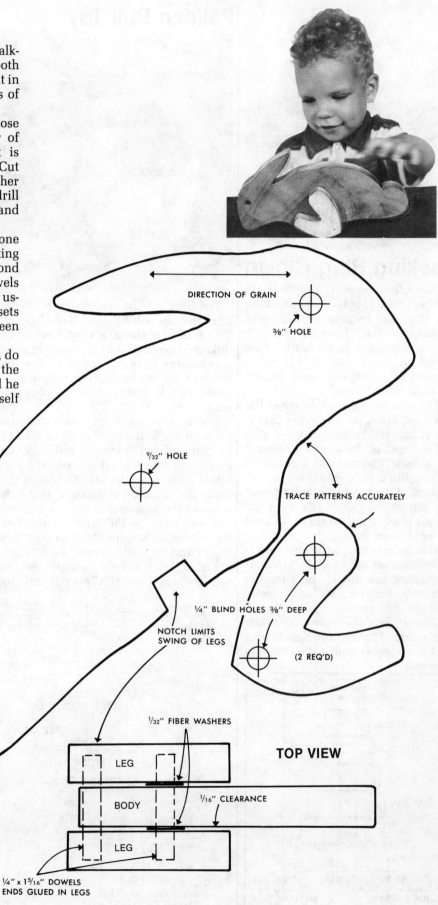

DIRECTION OF GRAIN

3/8" HOLE

9/32" HOLE

TRACE PATTERNS ACCURATELY

1/4" BLIND HOLES 3/8" DEEP

NOTCH LIMITS SWING OF LEGS

(2 REQ'D)

1/32" FIBER WASHERS

TOP VIEW

LEG

BODY

1/16" CLEARANCE

LEG

1/4" x 1 5/16" DOWELS
ENDS GLUED IN LEGS

Stacking Wagon Pull Toy

This popular toy teaches coordination and recognition of visual relationships as the child plays with it—and most importantly, it's fun for the child to assemble.

Hardwoods (recommended), softwoods or a combination of the two can be used. This is an ideal project for cleaning up your shop scrap pile.

We suggest that you gather the various pieces of different woods before you begin cutting. Assign shapes to the individual pieces of different woods according to the sizes of the stock available and the graining.

The fundamental dimension is 3-1/2 in. The square pieces are 3-1/2 in. on each side and the sanded doughnut wheels are 3-1/2 in. in diameter. The rectangular pieces with two holes are 3-1/2 x 7 in. and the main runners are 3-1/2 x 14 in. (holes 3-1/2 in. apart).

The two center holes in the runners have dowels glued into them. Use 7/8 or 1 in. dowels; determine height according to thickness of other component pieces.

The end holes in the runners slip over dowels glued vertically into the axles. The axles themselves are made of 1-1/2 in. square maple, with the ends turned a bit under 1 in. to accept the wheels. Smaller 3/8 in. dowels are used as keeper pins to hold the wheels in place on the axle.

All edges, especially those on exposed dowel ends, should be sanded and smoothed completely. Add the tow rope and handle (1 in. dowel) and the toy is ready for finishing. Use a good nontoxic sealer and varnish to complete your work.

Disassembled toy looks more complicated than it really is. Uniformity of dimensions simplifies construction.

First step in assembly clarifies entire procedure, helps child visualize relationship between pieces and final goal.

Lacing Boot Bank

Here's a one-evening project that can be duplicated dozens of times once the first pattern is made. It is a good gift shop item for a craftsman who wants to make a few dollars from his hobby, because in addition to being a handsome bank, it has the practical educational aspect as an aid to teaching a child to lace and tie shoes.

Scraps of almost any kind of wood can be used, since the finished project is painted. The one pictured was painted a bright red with white lacing. The latter can be an actual shoelace, heavy twine or yarn in a cclor that contrasts with that of the boot.

Enlarge the squared drawing to make patterns for the sides, and the edges of the front and back. Use stiff cardboard for the patterns, or even 1/8 in. hardboard if you want to use the patterns to make several banks.

A band saw does the job quickly, but an electric jig saw or even a hand scroll saw can be used to cut the profiles. Be sure to slightly round all cut edges with sandpaper to remove any roughness or splinters.

If you can't find corks for the hole in the bottom through which the money is recovered, bore a hole that is a snug fit for a short length of 1 in. dowel.

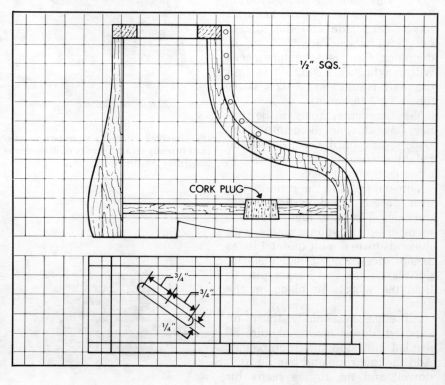

Tiny Tot's Rocking Horse

For some reason tiny tots will spend more time rocking than at practically any other form of play. This cartoonish little happy horse is sure to capture a little one's affections.

The first step in construction is to enlarge the squared drawings to make your patterns, then cut out the seat board, two runners and the head. If you use solid stock, be sure the grain runs the length of the several pieces to assure maximum strength. When softwood is used for the seat and runners, it's a good idea to use plywood for the horse head.

Use a coping saw, saber or band saw to cut the pieces, clamping the rockers together so they will be identical.

Sand all pieces thoroughly, using progressively finer grits to achieve a glass-smooth surface. Next, assemble the sanded rockers and seat board with glue and screws. Fasten the brace between the rockers, flush with the front of the seat board.

Leave the horse head off for the moment and apply a generous coat or two of sealer to the head and partly assembled rocker. Be sure the sealer and other finishing materials are nontoxic and "child-safe." Toddlers often chew on toys.

After the sealer has dried, paint on the eyes, mane and ears. Use black paint or a black felt-tip pen. The halter is bright red. When the patterns are dry, apply another coat of clear sealer.

When the sealer is dry, attach the head to the rocker with glue and screws. Bore the 5/8 in. hole and glue in the 5 in. length of dowel. Be sure to wipe away excess glue.

When the glue has set, apply several more coats of clear nontoxic sealer, sanding between each coat.

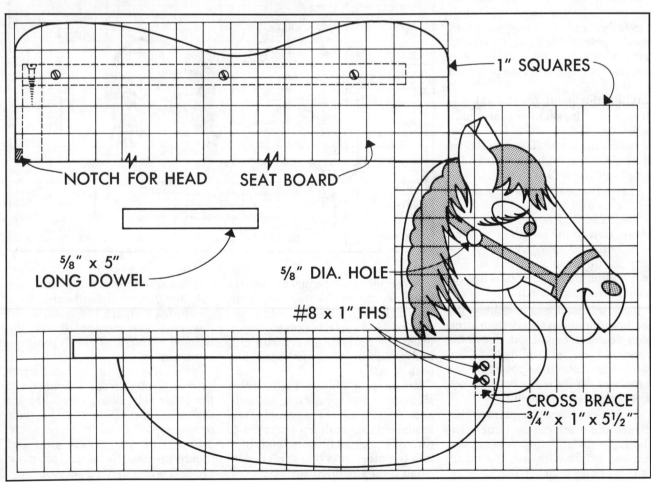

NOTCH FOR HEAD   SEAT BOARD

1" SQUARES

⅝" x 5" LONG DOWEL

⅝" DIA. HOLE

#8 x 1" FHS

CROSS BRACE
¾" x 1" x 5½"

Toddler Rocking Horse Chair

Even the smallest buckeroo will enjoy this old time "merry-go-round" horse. It actually is nothing more than a sturdy seat with rockers. A dowel is used both as a handhold for the child, and to keep him safely in place.

Additionally, a leather strap could be run from the center of the dowel, down to the center of the underside of the seat to prevent the child from sliding down and out.

The two sides are cut from 3/4 in. hardwood plywood. Make a pattern by enlarging the squared drawing, and be sure to mark the locations for the dowels, screws, seat and footboards.

Note that the handhold dowel and the stretcher dowels require blind holes 1/4 in. deep on the inside surfaces of the sides. A countersunk hole is bored from the outside surfaces of the sides so screws can be driven into the centers of the dowels. Similar holes are drilled for the screws that hold the seat and back.

Cut out the sides and bore the necessary holes. Sand all edges carefully, and fill any voids or rough spots. Final-sand, then paint both sides white. Be sure the paint you use for any part of the project is nontoxic.

While the paint on the sides is drying, cut the seat, back and footboard from 1/2 in. stock. Use 3/4 in. plywood for the seat, or use lighter stock if you prefer to keep down the weight of the rocker.

Fasten the seat and back together with glue and screws.

The handhold dowel is cut from 3/4 in. dowel, the length of the seat and footboard, plus 1/2 in. for the two 1/4 in. deep blind holes. The two bottom 1/2 in. stretchers are cut exactly the same length.

Paint the seat/back assembly, the footboard and the two bottom stretcher dowels a bright red. Leave the handhold dowel unfinished, but sand it as smooth as possible. The handhold dowel is the one the toddler might use for teething.

Go back to the white-painted side pieces and mark out the pattern for the horses. Paint the rockers, saddle and bridle with red; the mane, tail, eyes and trim are black.

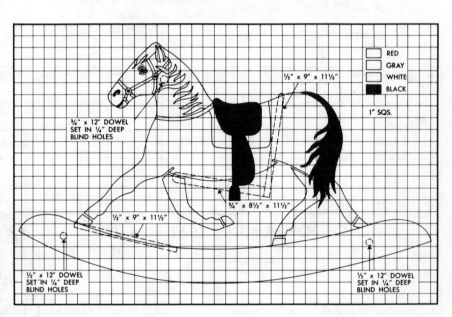

☐	RED
☐	GRAY
☐	WHITE
■	BLACK

1" SQS.

¾" x 12" DOWEL SET IN ¼" DEEP BLIND HOLES

½" x 9" x 11½"

¾" x 8½" x 11½"

½" x 9" x 11½"

½" x 12" DOWEL SET IN ¼" DEEP BLIND HOLES

½" x 12" DOWEL SET IN ¼" DEEP BLIND HOLES

Assembling all the pieces can be a bit tricky, so an assistant would be very helpful. Place one side down on a padded surface, outside down, insert the several dowels with glue and position the footboard and seat.

You may be able to fit the other side onto the projecting dowels, and over the seat assembly and footboard, but it might be easier to turn the assembly over and fit it into the other side that is placed inside up on a padded surface.

Drive screws into the dowels, and into the seat and footboard. It's a good idea to mark the positions of the seat and footboard on the painted surfaces to aid in positioning them.

Invert the assembly, and drive screws through from the outside of the other side, being careful to get the seat and footboard in their proper positions.

Clean off any excess glue and touch up any flaws in the paint created while driving screws.

Rocking Zebra

There are lots of rocking horses around, but the kid with the zebra is the envy of all his friends. And you'll get extra applause for building one (or you can make it a horse or pony from the same plan).

Hardly perceptible except to the experienced eye is a safety feature on the rockers themselves. Continuous arc rockers are fine for toddlers, but when an older child kicks the zebra into too hard a gallop it would be possible to rock completely over, either foward or backward.

For that reason the ends of the rockers are turned slightly down at the back and front to retard the rockers' travel. This would not, of course, prevent a child from being thrown forward or backward off the zebra if he or she was too rambunctious.

The rockers are made by striking off an arc with a radius of 33 in. for the outside curve and 31 in. for the inside curve to create rockers 2 in. high. The downward turn begins about 1-1/2 squares in from each end. The greater the downward curve, the better the snubbing action. Glue two pieces of 3/4 in. plywood together to make the stock. A straight-line measurement between the tips of the rockers measures 42 in. The idle zebra tilts forward slightly, but levels when a child gets aboard.

Note that dowels should run completely across between the rockers and through the legs, although they are not shown in the photo.

The black and white paint job makes the zebra. Merely alter the paint job to make a pinto, a dapple or some other colored horse.

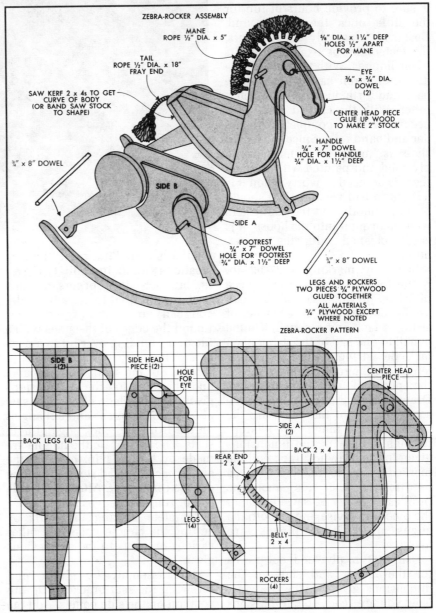

Two-Way Tot's
Teeter/Slide

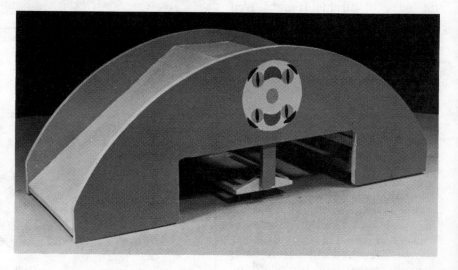

Here's an indoor/outdoor toy that is sure to provide hours of fun for the little ones the year 'round. Designed especially for toddlers, the teeter/slide is exactly what its name implies. With the curved side down, children can enjoy rocking back and forth, just like on a teeter-totter. With the curved side up, it becomes a slide, complete with ladder and hand rails. Since the teeter/slide is made of exterior-grade plywood and painted with enamel, there is no need to worry when it is left out in bad weather. If it should become muddy and the youngsters want to bring it into the house, it is easily cleaned with the garden hose.

Begin by marking a 27-1/2 in. radius for the side panels on a piece of 3/4 in. plywood. A compass can be fashioned out of a piece of string, a tack and a pencil. Tie the pencil to one end of the string, then tack the string, with the proper length for the radius, to the edge of the plywood on the centerline. Draw the arc, checking that the squared ends of the panel are the same. Now mark the "step-through," following the dimensions given in the drawing. Tack nail the marked piece to the piece to be used for the other side panel. The profiles can now be sawed. Clamp the pieces in a vise and smooth the edges until both pieces are identical.

Using 1/2 in. plywood, cut pieces for the ladder and slide to the dimensions given in the drawing. Now you are ready to cut the steps

for the ladder. First mark the step locations and 1/2 in. radii. Using a 1 in. bit, bore the corners at each center point used to mark the radii. You can now cut out the steps. Round the edges of the steps with a file or a rounding over bit in a portable router.

Next, cut the seats, bottom panel and handle to the dimensions given. Set the blade of a power saw at 53 and 90 degrees and cut angles on the front and back edge of both seats. The "grips" on the handle are made by boring 1 in. holes at the end of each marked slot and sawing out the remainder. After the handle is cut, round all edges smooth.

Complete making the parts by cutting the handle posts and other various brackets to the dimensions given.

Start assembly by gluing and screwing the seat brackets (D) into position on the side panels. Add the

panel brackets (B) and bottom panel bracket (C), making sure the bottom panel bracket is centered on the vertical centerline. Now glue and screw the handle posts into position.

With the side panels on edge, curved side up, attach the bottom panel. Now, run a bead of glue along the panel brackets and position the slide and ladder. Tap them snug against the bottom panel and counterbore holes in the locations shown. Secure the slide and ladder with screws, driving the screws deep enough so they can be filled.

Next attach the seats. Make sure that the front edge of each seat is flush with the side panels before installing permanently.

Lastly, secure the handle brackets to the handle using No. 6 x 1-1/4 in. roundhead screws. Now position and attach the assembly to the handle posts.

Fill and sand all edges and surfaces smooth, then apply a coat of sealer. When dry, lightly sand and paint the teeter/slide with colors of your choice. Give the slide several coats, sanding between coats to produce a smooth finish. After the paint has dried, you can paint the clown face. If you prefer, use large decals that are available at paint and wallpaper stores.

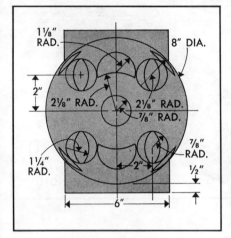

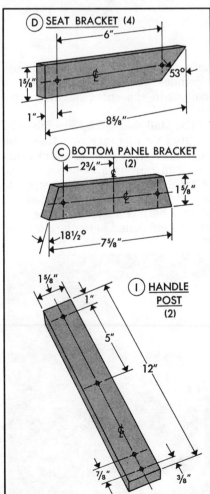

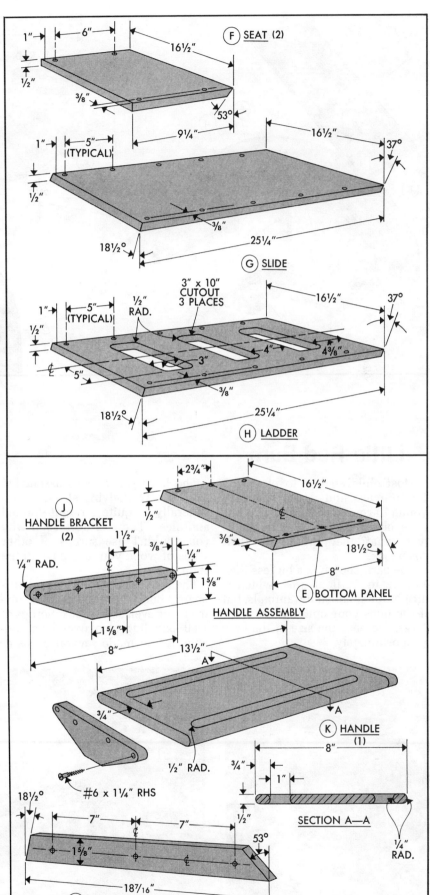

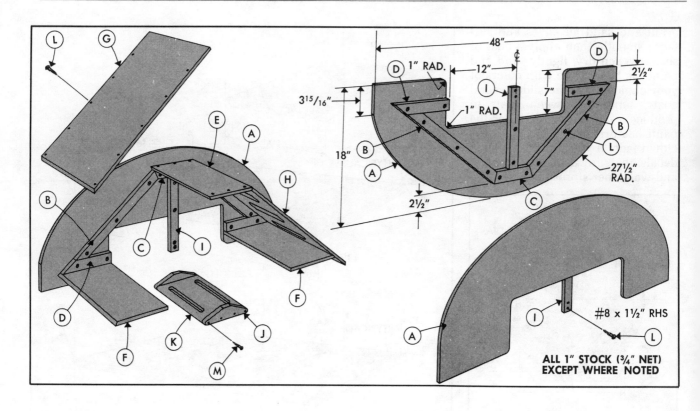

Little Red Barn

Most children like to play with toy animals, and if you have any young "farmers" in your family, this little old-fashioned barn might be just what they want for their "livestock."

The barn shown is a bit less than 10 x 12 in. in floor area, which is alright for smallish toy animals, but if the ones your children have are large, increase the size of the barn proportionately.

The barn shown was assembled from 1 x 12 shelving stock, which generally is quite straight-grained and clear. There is no reason why you couldn't use scraps of other kinds of wood you may have in the shop.

The roof is cut from 1/4 in. hardboard, but you might prefer plywood, or even solid stock. Scraps of wall paneling also would be suitable. If you made several barns as

gifts, it would be a good way to use up those wood scraps that seem to collect in the shop, but never get used.

The stall and ladder are made by ripping 1/4 x 1/4 in. strips, then joining them with popsicle sticks that you can purchase at hobby shops. Alternately, simply rip thin strips to about 1/8 in. thick and use them.

If the barn is made larger than the one dimensioned here, the stock for

the ladder and stall should be heavier than that shown in the drawing.

The stall and ladder are assembled with glue, no brads or nails being used. This eliminates the chance of snagging tiny fingers on nail or brad points.

Paint the barn bright red with a white roof. White is used to frame the door and simulate a sliding door, as indicated. White also is used for the windows painted on the ends of the barn. For a more realistic look, you might use strips of thin wood, as used for the ladder treads and stall, to frame the windows and door.

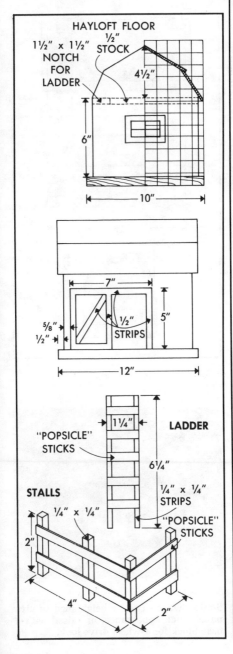

Miniature Wooden Toy Cars

Wooden toys have ageless appeal. They are fun and easy to make, children delight in playing with them, and they offer a refreshing change from their fragile plastic counterparts—well-crafted wooden toys should last a family through several generations of active use.

The toys shown here were built using two basic construction methods. The Volkswagen, van and station wagon were built from blocks of 4 x 4, with plywood bumpers and wheels added. The other vehicles were built up from 3/4 in. stock with various pieces added as shown.

Beginning toymakers sometimes are perplexed by the question of wheel making techniques. The wheels shown on these vehicles can be made any of several ways.

If large diameter dowels are available, you can slice off the wheels as required. If suitable doweling is unavailable in your area and you do not have a lathe, you may be able to have dowels turned at a nominal charge by a local cabinetmaker.

Another approach is to cut wood or plywood disks, using a fly-cutter or hole saw in a drill press. A hole saw in a portable drill will do an acceptable job.

If you do not have the materials, tools or desire to make wheels yourself, you can buy them. Purchased wheels will be slightly thicker than the plywood ones used here, but you can sand them to the desired thickness.

To make any of the 4 x 4 block-based toys, the first step is to cut the body to overall length. Next, cut the various side and top profiles shown. Cut the wheel-well arcs with a hole saw and use a chisel to cut away the scrap, or bore the wheel wells to exact depth and diameter (an expansive bit can be a real convenience for such jobs).

Drill axle holes in the wheels and body, then insert 3/8 in. dowel axles. The holes for the axles should be slightly oversize, and the axle centers should be lightly waxed to assure smooth turning. Mount washers as spacers outside the body on the axles and glue the wheels on the axle ends.

To make the built-up vehicles, cut the necessary components for each and mark the pieces for identification. Assembly is straight glue and clamp, but we do recommend that you assemble the center sections first, working from the bottom up. Follow the same wheel mounting procedures as for the 4 x 4 toys.

All wooden toys should be thoroughly sanded, with particular attention given to the corners and edges. If you want the bright colors and protection offered by enamel, be sure to select a child-safe, nontoxic type.

Here are a few tips on construction of the individual toys:

Volkswagen. Cut a slanted kerf for the windshield (lower edge approximately 1-1/2 in. from the front edge of the body) before cutting the curved and slanted profiles.

Van/Bus. Cut the slanted sides (window areas), then cut the front.

Station Wagon. Cut the side window areas, kerf for the windshield, then complete the front "notch" by cutting across the hood area.

Semi-Tractor and Trailer. Make the trailer first, then cut and assemble all the tractor except the pivot block for the trailer. Place the trailer's hitch in the pivot block, hold the block in place on the tractor, and move the trailer from side to side; the front of the trailer should clear the back of the cab. If the pivot action is unrestricted, attach the block as shown; otherwise, move the block back as required or cut and drill another one to fit.

Jeep. To simplify assembly, you can modify the plans to provide for a folded-down windshield.

Pickup Truck and Camper. If you have any true 4 x 4 in. (net) stock, you can use it for a closed camper to simplify construction design.

Jeep is as distinctive as Volkswagen; "peg people" can have green helmets and uniforms for a military version.

Van/bus has slightly-angled side window areas; for a more emphatic and readily identifiable look, paint on "windows."

Volkswagen's shape is ideal for a wooden toy—a distinctive profile incorporating swept, curved lines.

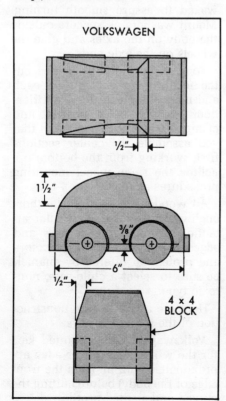

VOLKSWAGEN

6"

1½"

3/8"

½"

4 x 4 BLOCK

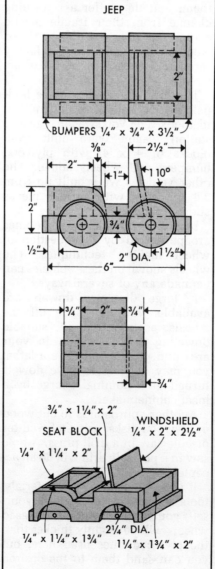

JEEP

BUMPERS ¼" x ¾" x 3½"

3/8" — 2½"
2" — 1"
10°
2"
¾"
½"
2" DIA. — 1½"
6"

¾" — 2" — ¾"
¾"

¾" x 1¼" x 2"
SEAT BLOCK
WINDSHIELD
¼" x 2" x 2½"
¼" x 1¼" x 2"
2¼" DIA.
¼" x 1¼" x 1¾"
1¼" x 1¾" x 2"

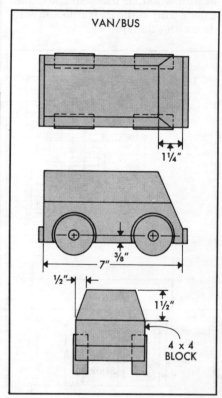

VAN/BUS

1¼"

7"
3/8"

½"
1½"
4 x 4 BLOCK

Station wagon can be heightened to give panel truck appearance, or raised with a base block for 4-wheel drive look.

STATION WAGON

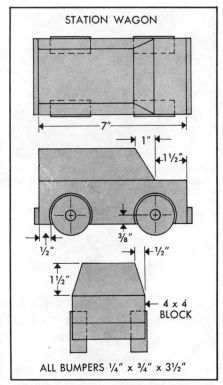

ALL BUMPERS 1/4" x 3/4" x 3 1/2"

Tractor-trailer combination has the powerful, husky look of the real thing.

SEMI TRAILER

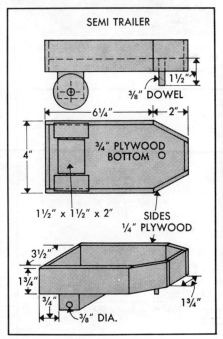

3/8" DOWEL

3/4" PLYWOOD BOTTOM

1 1/2" x 1 1/2" x 2"

SIDES 1/4" PLYWOOD

3/8" DIA.

SEMI TRACTOR

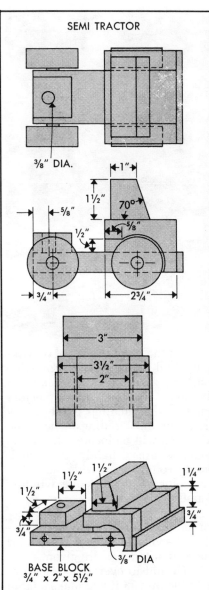

3/8" DIA.

BASE BLOCK 3/4" x 2" x 5 1/2"

3/8" DIA

Pickup with removable camper invites addition of boat and trailer; modify semi-trailer plans to suit.

PICKUP TRUCK

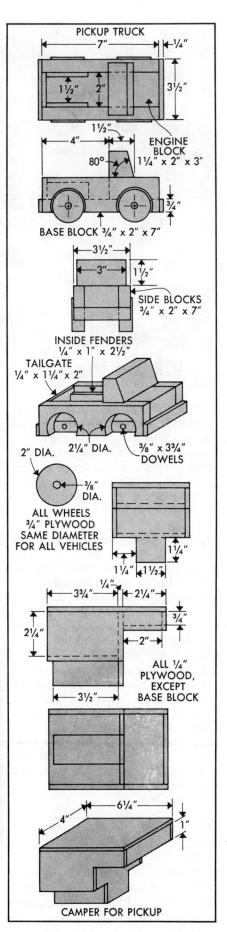

ENGINE BLOCK 1 1/4" x 2" x 3"

BASE BLOCK 3/4" x 2" x 7"

SIDE BLOCKS 3/4" x 2" x 7"

INSIDE FENDERS 1/4" x 1" x 2 1/2"

TAILGATE 1/4" x 1 1/4" x 2"

2" DIA.   2 1/4" DIA.   3/8" x 3 3/4" DOWELS

3/8" DIA.

ALL WHEELS 3/4" PLYWOOD SAME DIAMETER FOR ALL VEHICLES

ALL 1/4" PLYWOOD, EXCEPT BASE BLOCK

CAMPER FOR PICKUP

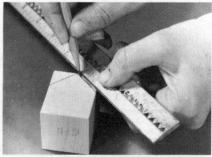

Mark roof angles on end of building as indicated in diagram, showing side view of individual building.

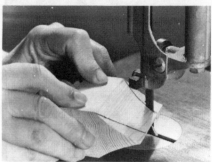

For two-angle roofs, cut first set, then mark and cut second. Hold flat surface down firmly as you feed into blade.

Sand all surfaces thoroughly, then glue together parts of buildings made from more than one block.

Village Blocks

To a small child this little storybook village is a fascinating source for hours of imaginative play. The buildings were inspired by old fashioned European wooden toys that used to fill Christmas stockings.

Use pine blocks of three thicknesses, 3/4 in., 1-1/8 in. and 1-1/2 in., to make the buildings. Be sure you make no buildings small enough for a child to put in his mouth and choke on. This is no toy for tiny tots who will view the buildings as chewables. Cut blocks to size from the proper thickness for each building, then shape roofs to fit. Some buildings are shaped from single blocks, some built up.

Cut the blocks to the dimensions given in the diagrams and mark the roof angles as indicated in the side view of each building. Saw roof to shape. In some instances, a roof may have two sets of angles; after sawing the first set, mark the second one. Hold the building firmly on the saw table and feed the peak into the blade.

Sand all surfaces smooth, then glue together the parts of those buildings made from more than one block. Use any good non-toxic finish to paint the surfaces a solid color or to antique them so they will resemble their original European counterparts.

When the paint dries, put on windows and doors with an indelible marking pen. If you desire a "lighted" window effect, *before painting the buildings* paint yellow areas on the buildings where the windows will be located. Mark the window areas lightly in pencil, paint around them with the building color, then mark the window details with pen.

Add people and trees lathe-turned from birch or maple to complete the village. Several designs for these final touches are given.

You'll add to everyone's pleasure with the project if you make a large "village hall" toy box for storage. Scale up the design for House K, use 3/4 in. plywood for the shell, hinge the roof and attach a handle.

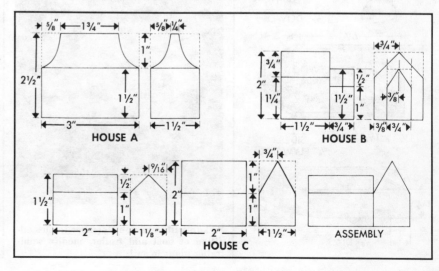

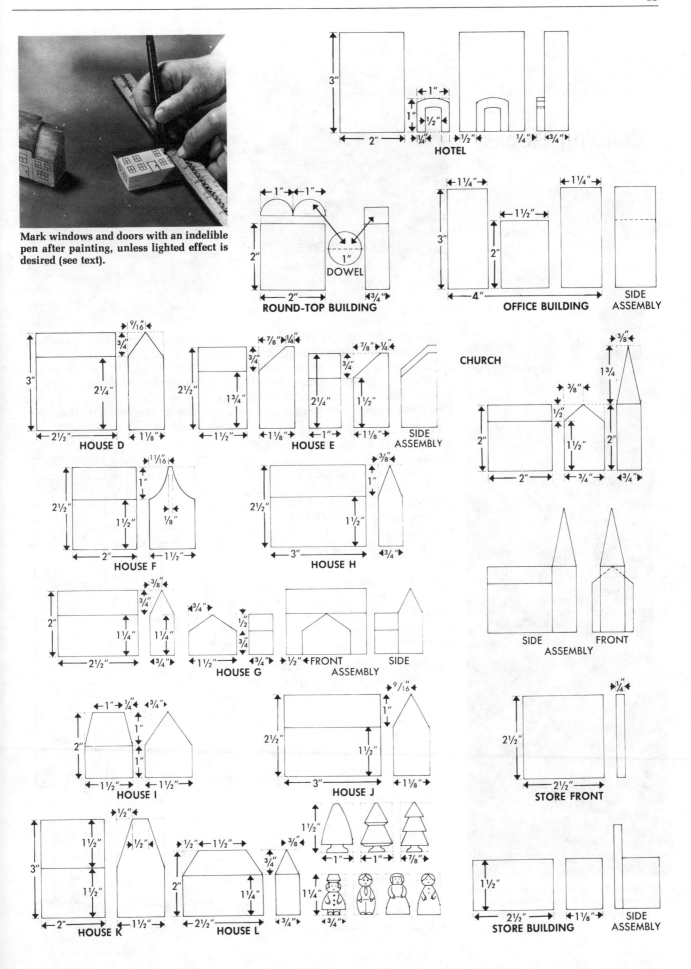

Mark windows and doors with an indelible pen after painting, unless lighted effect is desired (see text).

HOTEL

ROUND-TOP BUILDING
DOWEL

OFFICE BUILDING
SIDE ASSEMBLY

HOUSE D

HOUSE E
SIDE ASSEMBLY

HOUSE F

HOUSE H

CHURCH
SIDE ASSEMBLY
FRONT

HOUSE G
FRONT ASSEMBLY
SIDE

HOUSE I

HOUSE J

STORE FRONT

HOUSE K

HOUSE L

STORE BUILDING
SIDE ASSEMBLY

Building Blocks

Building blocks are as old as toys, as young as tomorrow. Make them from scrap wood, give your youngsters years of constructive fun.

Generations of American children have had hours of fun building log houses, forts and even modern skyscrapers with these simple blocks. Here's a genuine "fun" toy that fosters creativity in children.

Oak was used in the original blocks; this tough material lasts longer than most woods, but maple or other close-grained hardwood can be substituted. Start by ripping the stock into 1/4 x 1-3/4 in. strips. Cut the blocks to length before cutting the notches. A dado blade set at 5/16 in. will simplify cutting the notches.

A hole is drilled in the top piece for a flag pole. The flag is the type used on a bicycle and can be obtained at many hardware and novelty stores.

Hone off all the sharp edges on the blocks with sandpaper, then stain them, over which nontoxic varnish is applied. You also can enamel the blocks in various colors if a particular child is more intrigued by bright colors, and more attracted to the modern than pioneer buildings.

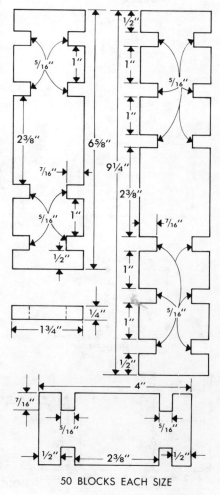

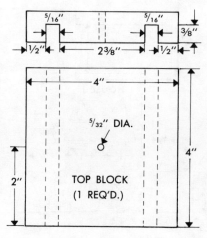

50 BLOCKS EACH SIZE

Gravity Marble Game

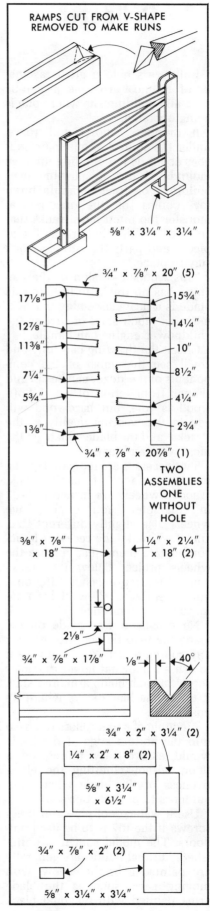

RAMPS CUT FROM V-SHAPE REMOVED TO MAKE RUNS

5/8" x 3¼" x 3¼"

¾" x ⅞" x 20" (5)

17⅛"   15¾"
12⅞"   14¼"
11⅜"   10"
7¼"   8½"
5¾"   4¼"
1⅜"   2¾"

¾" x ⅞" x 20⅞" (1)

TWO ASSEMBLIES ONE WITHOUT HOLE

⅜" x ⅞" x 18"   ¼" x 2¼" x 18" (2)

2⅛"

¾" x ⅞" x 17⅞"   ⅛"   40°

¾" x 2" x 3¼" (2)

¼" x 2" x 8" (2)

⅝" x 3¼" x 6½"

¾" x ⅞" x 2" (2)

⅝" x 3¼" x 3¼"

This simple game that consists of marbles rolling down slanting ramps continues to fascinate both young and old.

Construction is quite easy, with the only challenge being the cutting of the V-channels in the marble runs. On a table saw, set the blade at 40 degrees and lower it until it projects just 5/8 in. above the table. Move the rip fence over to 1/8 in. from the blade.

Using a push stick and a hold-down stick for added safety, run the 3/4 x 7/8 in. strips over the saw in one direction, then reverse each strip and run it back in the other direction. A V-shape strip should fall loose.

Assemble the end "towers" from the designated strips and bore a hole near the bottom of one to allow the marbles to exit into the box.

Use the scrap V-shape pieces to make small "ramps" to insert in the upper end of each run. They speed up the marbles and prevent a row of marbles from dropping on each other.

To make the ramps, cut a 45 degree angle about 1/2 in. from the end of the V-strip, then saw at right angles about 1/2 in. from the angle cut. You will need five of the ramps, which are glued and held with a single countersunk brad in the high end of each run.

Build the box in which the marbles collect, then glue in the two small blocks that position the bottom of the tower and also prevent the marbles from rolling into the small areas beside the bottom of the tower.

Fit one tower with a base 3-1/4 in. square. Mark on each tower the locations of the runs, then glue and brad the runs to the insides of the towers. Note that the high end of each run fits to the back of the towers, while the low ends are spaced to allow the marbles to drop between the ends of the runs and the backs of the towers.

Finish the game with bright colors for little youngsters, a stain and varnish being more practical for older children.

Bulldozer

Bulldozers hold a great fascination for almost everyone, as can be seen at a building site where one is being operated.

It thunders, snorts and roars, under the control of one man, as it goes about its job of piling up huge mounds of dirt or pushing over buildings or trees. Manufactured toy copies of the mechanical monster too often have tracks that come off, blades that break off and pieces and parts that simply won't stay in place.

This wooden version of the machine has no tracks to lose and its blade is a heavy assembly that will move as much sand or dirt as the childpower engine can handle.

Check the drawing carefully and you'll see that most of the components of the 'dozer can be cut and shaped from scraps of wood. Softwood is fine, but hardwood will add to the wearing quality of the "tracks" and the blade which get the most wear and tear.

Two recesses are indicated on the inside surface of each track. Wooden wheels are turned to 2-1/2 in. diameter. You might have wheels of a slightly different size, and if so, make the recesses to accommodate them. Just be sure the wheels project below the tracks enough to assure easy rolling on a bumpy surface. Allow at least 1/4 in. to 1/2 in. clearance.

No provision was made on the blade for it to be held up, nor for any rolling assist. You might want to use a somewhat larger diameter screw in each blade arm, and snug it up so the blade stays where it's positioned.

A couple of small rollers recessed into the bottom edge of the blade would assure easy rolling on a floor, without limiting the effectiveness of the blade when used outdoors to push dirt or sand.

Use a waterproof glue and brass screws if the toy is to be used outdoors. The model shown is unfinished, but real bulldozers generally are painted a bright yellow, with moving parts such as the blade arms painted with diagonal black

stripes as a safety measure. The back of the rig also has the diagonal black stripes.

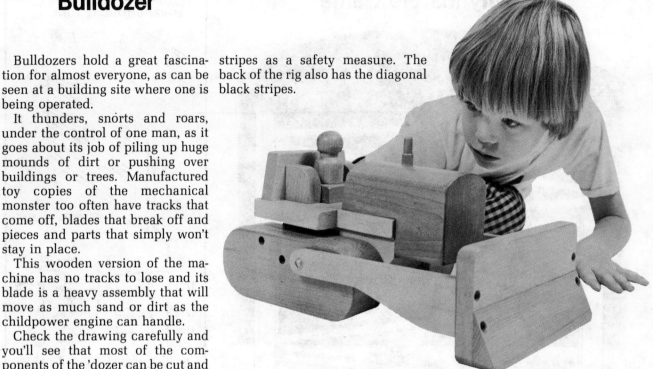

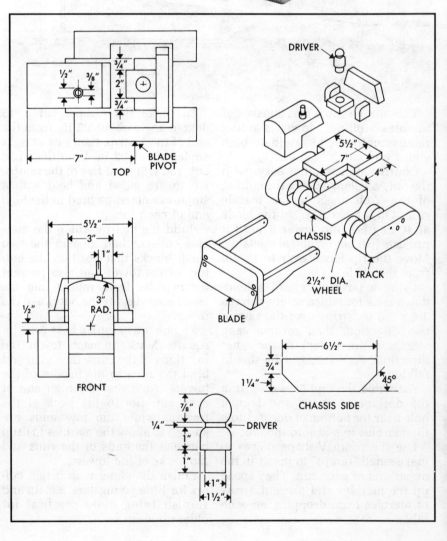

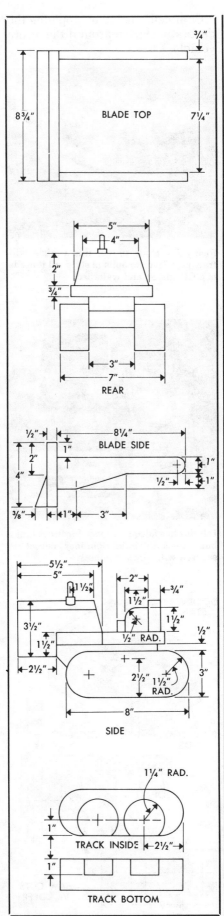

Dump Truck

Pieces of 1 and 2 in. stock from the scrap box are used to make this action toy in just an hour or two.

Cut the "chassis" from a piece of 1 x 4 and notch the end as shown. Drill a 3/8 in. hole through the chassis across the notch.

The "hood" of the truck is a piece of 2 x 4 with the front edge beveled as indicated then glued and nailed to the chassis. Slice two 1/4 in. sections from a 1/2 in. dowel to make headlights that are glued and bradded to the front.

The "cab" is a block of wood notched as shown. This can be done on a table or radial arm saw with a dado blade, or you can use a handsaw to make four cuts, then chisel out the waste between the four posts. The top of the cab is beveled on the front edge, and glued and bradded to the posts.

The dump body is made of 1/2 or 3/4 in. stock—whatever is in the scrap box—to the dimensions given. A small piece of 1 in. scrap (3/4 in. net) is cut to make the "tilt block" that is drilled for the 3/8 in. dowel that fits through the notch in the chassis. The "tail gate" of the truck is held only by two screws at the top that let it swing open when the truck body is tilted, so the cargo is dumped.

Wheels are cut or turned from 1 and 2 in. stock. Use a fly cutter in a drill press, or a hole saw in a portable electric drill.

Paint the finished truck with lead-free enamels in bright colors.

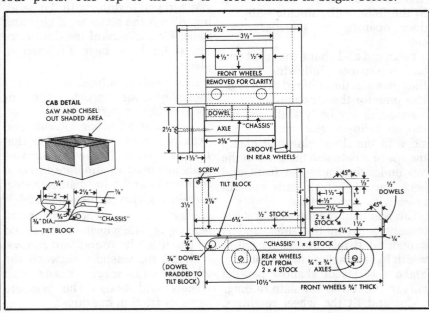

Complete the job by applying the decorative stripe around the entire vehicle.

Ready for show or go, this vehicle will transport favorite dolls in style; all it needs is a CB, stereo and waterbed.

Motor Home

Little boys especially will be thrilled to play with this scaled down version of a motor home.

Use solid-core birch plywood for most of the construction. This material has a good dense surface that accepts paint very well. Whatever material you choose should have a comparable surface.

Start work by cutting the sides to size. Lay out the perimeters of the door and window openings and cut them. For clean, splinter-free cuts, tape over all marked lines first and keep the good side of the plywood up. Cut wheel-well openings in the sides and clean up all edges.

The floor should be cut next. Make certain that the stair opening in the floor will coincide with the door opening on the passenger side.

Next, cut and shape the front and back top spacers, following the profiles given in the squared drawings. Use pine for these components.

Assemble the body shell, less the top, as follows: glue and nail the sides to the floor, glue and clamp the spacers between the sides at the top ends, then add the front and back panels. Set all nails and fill holes with a wood filler.

Cut and trim the top so that it fits loosely between the sides and is supported firmly across its entire width by the rabbets in the spacers. Make a series of shallow parallel cuts in the top to simulate ribbing.

Cut and fit the wheel retainers, window and door trim. The retainers are mounted inside the sides and flush with the side-bottom edges, where they are glued and clamped. Glue and brad the window and door trim in place.

To complete the main assembly, cut and fit the interior room dividers and attach them with glue and brads. Set the assembly aside, cut and fit (but do not attach) all remaining components, then sand all pieces and paint as desired. Preferably use good, hard enamels for the body and trim, and wait to apply the decorative "wraparound" stripe until all other remaining steps have been completed.

When you're done with the painting, attach the stairs with glue and nails. Fit and mount the door after the stairs have been fastened in place.

Use contact adhesive to apply indoor-outdoor carpet scraps or some other material to the floor, then mount all other interior and exterior pieces as shown. Note that 1 in. diameter hardwood drawer pulls are used to simulate forward roof vents and 1 in. diameter steel furniture glides for headlights.

Also note the wheel mounting technique. The wheels are mounted on No. 10 x 2 in. roundhead screws, with 1/4 in. washers between the wheels and screw heads and wheels and body. The washers serve as friction bearings.

Interior has adequate space for furnishings built to suit; indoor-outdoor carpet is secured with contact adhesive.

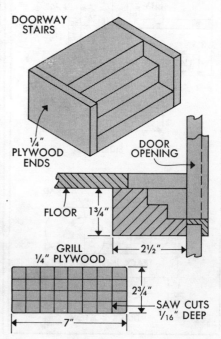

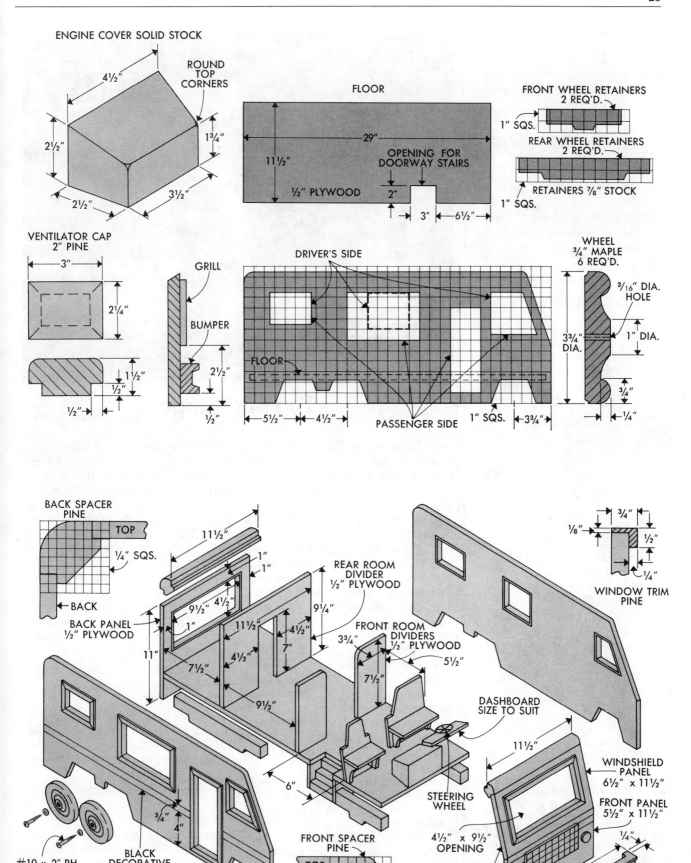

ENGINE COVER SOLID STOCK

ROUND TOP CORNERS

4½"
2½"
2½"
3½"
1¾"

FLOOR

29"
11½"
½" PLYWOOD
OPENING FOR DOORWAY STAIRS
2"
3"
6½"

FRONT WHEEL RETAINERS
2 REQ'D.
1" SQS.

REAR WHEEL RETAINERS
2 REQ'D.
RETAINERS ⅞" STOCK
1" SQS.

VENTILATOR CAP
2" PINE
3"
2¼"
1½"
½"
½"

GRILL

BUMPER
2½"
½"

DRIVER'S SIDE

FLOOR

5½"
4½"
1" SQS.
3¾"
PASSENGER SIDE

WHEEL
¾" MAPLE
6 REQ'D.
3/16" DIA. HOLE
1" DIA.
3¾" DIA.
¾"
¼"

BACK SPACER
PINE
TOP
¼" SQS.
BACK
BACK PANEL
½" PLYWOOD

WINDOW TRIM
PINE
¾"
⅛"
½"
¼"

11½"
1"
1"
9½"
4½"
1"
11½"
4½"
4½"
7½"
9½"
11"

REAR ROOM DIVIDER
½" PLYWOOD
9¼"

FRONT ROOM DIVIDERS
½" PLYWOOD
3¾"
5½"
7½"
7"

DASHBOARD
SIZE TO SUIT

WINDSHIELD PANEL
6½" x 11½"

FRONT PANEL
5½" x 11½"

11½"

6"
¾"
4"

#10 x 2" RH SCREWS
BLACK DECORATIVE STRIPE
¼" WASHER
PASSENGER SIDE

FRONT SPACER
PINE
TOP
¼" SQS.
WINDSHIELD

STEERING WHEEL

4½" x 9½"
OPENING
½" PLYWOOD
HEADLIGHT
BUMPER
SOLID STOCK
11¼"
3"
¾"
12½"
¼"
¼" SQS.
BUMPER

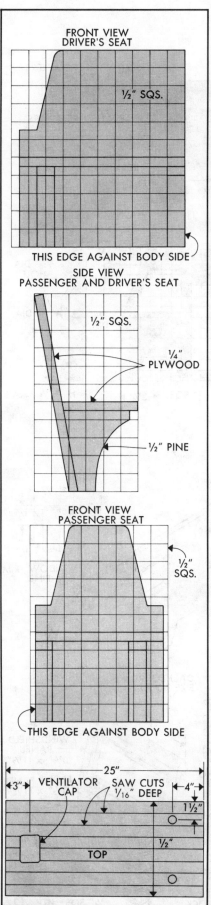

**FRONT VIEW
DRIVER'S SEAT**

½" SQS.

THIS EDGE AGAINST BODY SIDE

**SIDE VIEW
PASSENGER AND DRIVER'S SEAT**

½" SQS.

¼" PLYWOOD

½" PINE

**FRONT VIEW
PASSENGER SEAT**

½" SQS.

THIS EDGE AGAINST BODY SIDE

25"

3"

VENTILATOR CAP

SAW CUTS 1/16" DEEP

4"

1½"

TOP

½"

Tug and Barge

Children enjoy simple toys they can push around on the floor, and over which they have complete control. Boats have a particular fascination. This tug and barge set will provide years of fun for youngsters.

If softwood is used for the set, 1-1/2 in. stair lumber is ideal. Hardwood is a better bet for appearance and resistance to the battering the toys will get if used outdoors. Maple or birch are excellent for the purpose.

For the tug, cut a paper template and use it to mark out the hull shape on a block 1-1/2 x 5-1/2 x 11-1/2 in. Lightly pencil in a center line from bow to stern to aid in positioning the above-deck structures later.

Saw out the hull, then sand the sides smooth. The rounded front of the bridge roof can be cut next.

Now, cut the cabin and bridge sections from 1-1/2 x 2-1/2 in. stock. Be sure to cut both ends of the bridge, and one end of the cabin, at a 10 degree angle. Check the two pieces to make sure the angles are exact and that they mate properly. That is, that the front of the cabin and the back of the bridge meet in a tight joint. Sand a bit if necessary to create a neat fit.

Bore the hole in the cabin 1 in. diameter and 3/4 in. deep to accept the stack. Note that this also is raked back at a 10 degree angle. Cut the stack from a piece of 1 in. dowel, making it about 3-7/8 in. long. Sand the top at an angle to be parallel to the deck, which will bring it down to a height approximately 3 in. above the top of the cabin.

Sand all parts smooth, then use glue and nails to assemble. Countersunk screws will create a stronger assembly.

You may want to make several barges so they can be hooked up in a "barge train."

Note that this is an "ocean-going" tug, rather than a river tug. The latter have blunt bows and they push a "tow" of barges rather than pulling them as do ocean tugs.

Each rectangular barge has a 10 degree angle at bow and stern. Bore the 3/8 in. holes 3/4 in. deep near each corner. Sand all surfaces and round off all sharp edges. Glue the dowel bridle posts in the holes and, when the glue has set, round off the tops of the posts with sandpaper.

If a toddler is to use the tug and barge, shorten the stack on the tug and round the top. Also shorten the bridle posts on the barge so they project only about 1 in., and sand the tops round and smooth.

Drive a screw eye into the stern of the tug and attach a tow line such as nylon cord. Make a loop in the end of the cord so it can be dropped over the bridle post on the barge.

If several barges are to be "towed," make a line for each pair of barges, with loops at both ends of the line.

Paint the tug and the barge in bright colors with nontoxic, lead-free enamel. Most such paints will have a "child-safe" listing on the label.

Biplane

Your little aviator will be scanning the skies for a chance to take on the Red Baron or imitate the aerobatics of a barnstorming daredevil if you build this sturdy little airplane. Reminiscent of the Spad or Sopwith Camel of World War I, this rugged biplane is designed to stand up to the roughest of pilots and the worst of landing fields.

Its constantly spinning plexiglass propeller is not easy to break, yet it presents no hazard.

All parts of the plane can be easily shaped with hand tools, except the cowling at the front, which requires some whittling, filing and sanding. A lathe would permit shaping the cowling in a matter of minutes.

You can make patterns for the component parts by enlarging the squared drawings.

The cross section of the fuselage behind the cowling is an octagon with the corner surfaces a bit shorter than the top, bottom and sides. After shaping the octagon the full length of a stick 2 in. square and 8 in. long, the sides are angled back to create a 1 in. width at the back end of the fuselage. A notch is cut for the bottom wing and slots for the tail assembly.

The cowling is attached to the forward end of the fuselage with glue and two screws driven into the two counterbored holes in the cowling.

The rugged landing gear is a block shaped as indicated, to which the 1/2 x 1 in. diameter wheels are attached. The bottom wing is attached next, then the landing gear is fastened to it.

The strut for the top wing is cut to shape and glued and screwed to the fuselage, then the top wing is attached.

Shape the rudder and elevators and attach them to the fuselage. A "whirling propeller," actually a 1/4 x 4 in. circle of clear plexiglass with edges sanded round and smooth, is center-bored and screwed to the nose of the plane. Finally paint the plane as a World War I replica or perhaps with a brighter color of an air show daredevil's plane.

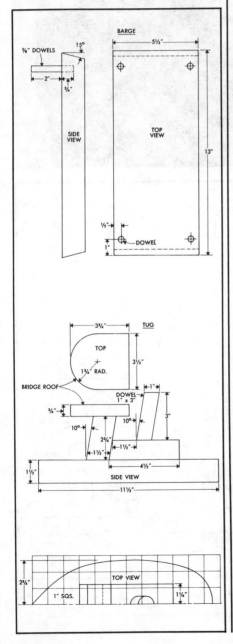

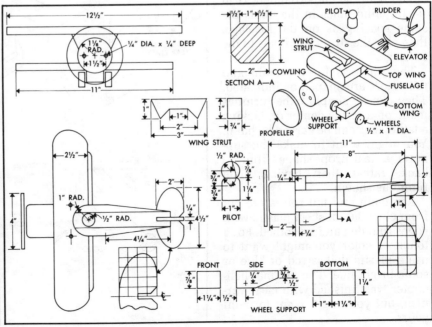

Helicopter

While this toy helicopter is as modern as today, its construction is as basic as toy building blocks, and you can create a dozen if a fleet of the "choppers" is needed to outfit the neighborhood youngsters.

A hardwood or softwood 4 x 4 is the stock used. Start by cutting off the four corners of a 10 in. length of 4 x 4 (or several pieces of 1 in. stock glued up to make a block) to 45 degrees x 1 in. A bit more or less than 1 in. will cause no problems.

Mark the back from the front end of the block 4-3/4 in. and cut a 45 degree notch at the top and bottom of the block. The top then is cut straight back to the tail end of the fuselage, while the bottom is cut at an angle to create a length of 3/4 in. at the end, as shown on the drawing.

The sides are cut at an angle, equally, to produce a width of 1 in. at the tail end of the fuselage. The nose of the fuselage now is cut and sanded as indicated to create the streamlined shape.

Drill the four holes in the lower angles of the fuselage for the struts that support the floats, centering them on the angled surface.

The floats are lengths of 1 in. dowel with the ends rounded. Drill 1/4 in. blind holes in the floats the same spacing as on the fuselage, then glue the struts and floats to the fuselage.

The supports for the main and tail rotors are shaped as indicated. They can be simple lathe turnings made on a screw center or, lacking a lathe, they can be carved by hand. You might want to make the supports a tear-drop shape front to back, rather than having them round as shown.

The main and tail rotors are cut from clear 3/8 in. sheet plastic with edges rounded and smoothed. For a touch of color you might want to use a plastic that is red or blue or some bright hue. The original helicopter was finished with clear varnish, but you might want to paint yours.

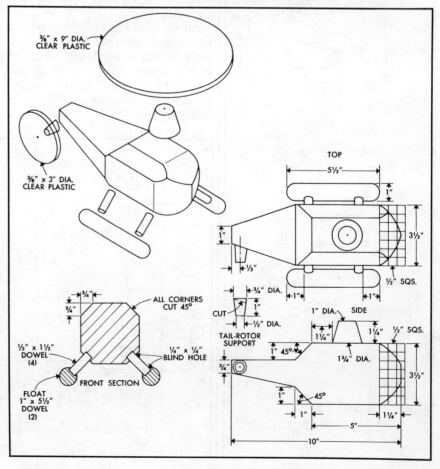

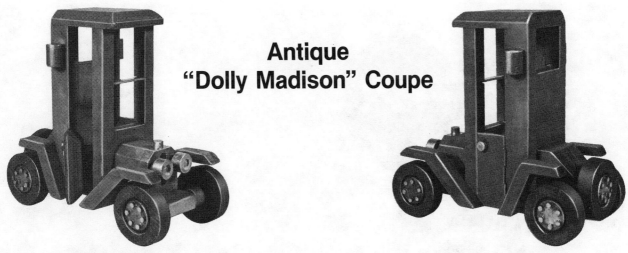

Antique "Dolly Madison" Coupe

Children of all ages will love this novel toy, and when well made it will last several generations. Only hand tools are required, although power tools will permit "mass-production" of the coupe if you wish to make a number for gifts.

Pine or other straight grained softwood is best. Cut all the pieces to size and shape, then start assembly by gluing together the three pieces (3) that form the trunk. Next, glue the dash panel (4) to the hood and radiator (1, 2) and the seat back (5) to the trunk. Glue the seat blocks together (6, 7) and to the seat back. Install the steering wheel post and steering wheel. Glue trunk and seat assembly to the chassis (8), then attach the doors with glue-soaked strips of denim, fitting pieces of waxed paper or aluminum foil between the folds to prevent their adhering together. When the glue is dry, pivot the doors to loosen the hinges, then assemble the rest of the car.

The finished car is sanded and all edges rounded. Apply antiquing or paint with bright colored, nontoxic enamels.

Materials List

All 1" pine (3/4" net)

1. 2-1/4" x 2-1/4" (2)
1A. 3/4" x 3/4" (2)
2. 2-1/4" x 2-1/4" (1)
3. 2-1/4" x 2-1/4" (3)
4. 2-1/4" x 2-7/8" (1
5. 2-1/4" x 6" (1)
6. 1" x 2-1/4" (1)
7. 7/8" x 2-1/4" (1)
8. 2-1/4" x 9-3/4" (1)
9. 1-3/4" x 2-7/8" (2)
10. 3-3/4" x 4-1/2" (1)
11. 1/2" x 2-7/8" (2)
12. 3/4" x 3" (2)
13. 3/4" x 2-1/2" (2)
14. 1/2" x 2-1/2" (2)
15. 1-3/8" x 8-3/4" (2)
16. 3/4" x 8-3/4" (2)
17. 1/8" x 1/2" x 2-5/8" (1)
18. 2-7/8" dia. disk (5)

Hardwood Dowels

19. 1/2" x 5" (2)
20. 3/4" x 1" dia. (4)
21. 1/2" dia. x 1" (2)
22. 5/8" x 1" dia. (2)
23. 1/2" dia. x 1" (1)
24. 1/4" x 1" dia. (1)
25. 1/2" dia. x 1" (1)
26. 1" dia. x 1-1/8" (2)
27. 1/2" dia. x 1/4" (2)
28. 1/2" dia. x 1/2" (1)
29. 1/4" dia. x 1/4" (30 – 6 each wheel)

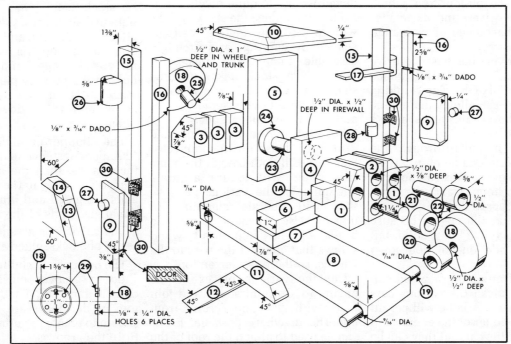

Junior Steam Train

Steam locomotives are described by the number of large drive wheels and the smaller, auxiliary wheels. For example, a big long haul engine might be an "eight-four-two" which means eight drivers and six smaller wheels, either ahead of or behind the drivers.

This yard engine has six drive wheels, and no auxiliaries, hence it's called a "Six-Oh." The resulting short wheelbase allows the engine to run on short-radius turns, as in a railroad yard.

The car it pulls through the switching yard can be of any type, but we've shown a tank car, box car, gondola or hopper and the ever-present caboose. There is no coal tender behind the engine because it's not a "play car" to a child, but you might add one of your own design.

Scraps of any kind of wood can be used to make the various cars and the engine. A lathe will permit turning the boiler of the engine and the tank for the car, but they can be whittled, filed and sanded to shape with hand tools.

Wheels are 1-1/8 in. in diameter, but 1/2 in. slices of 1 or 1-1/4 in. dowel would do quite nicely.

The two domes, the stack and the whistle on the engine can be shaped by carving, or you might assemble them from pieces of dowel. The stack has a tapered shape, but you can use a piece of straight dowel with some loss of authenticity in appearance.

Stack all the engine wheels and drill screw holes for the connector bar, and drill both bars at the same time. This will assure accurate alignment of the various parts so they will operate smoothly in unison. Use washers under the heads of the roundhead wood screws that connect the bars to the wheels, so there is easy action.

Cut the various pieces of the engine to size and shape and join them with glue and screws from underneath where possible. Brads can be used to attach the roof of the engine cab. Countersink them and cover the heads with wood putty.

The chassis of all the cars is the same size, 3-1/2 x 9 in., cut from 1 in. stock, 3/4 in. net. The tank is flattened slightly on the bottom and attached with glue and screws. The dome at the top is a length of 1-1/2 in. dowel shaped and fitted in a hole in the tank. A piece of 1/2 in. stock 2-1/4 in. square is center bored and fitted down over the dome.

The hopper/gondola has the "dumpers" fastened to the bottom of the chassis, then the sides are attached vertically to the top, and the ends are glued and bradded inside the angled ends of the sides.

The caboose is assembled from a series of blocks, glued and bradded.

The box car has sliding doors that slide in grooves chiseled in the chassis and roof. The top and bottom of the doors are rabbeted as shown to create the projections that fit in the grooves.

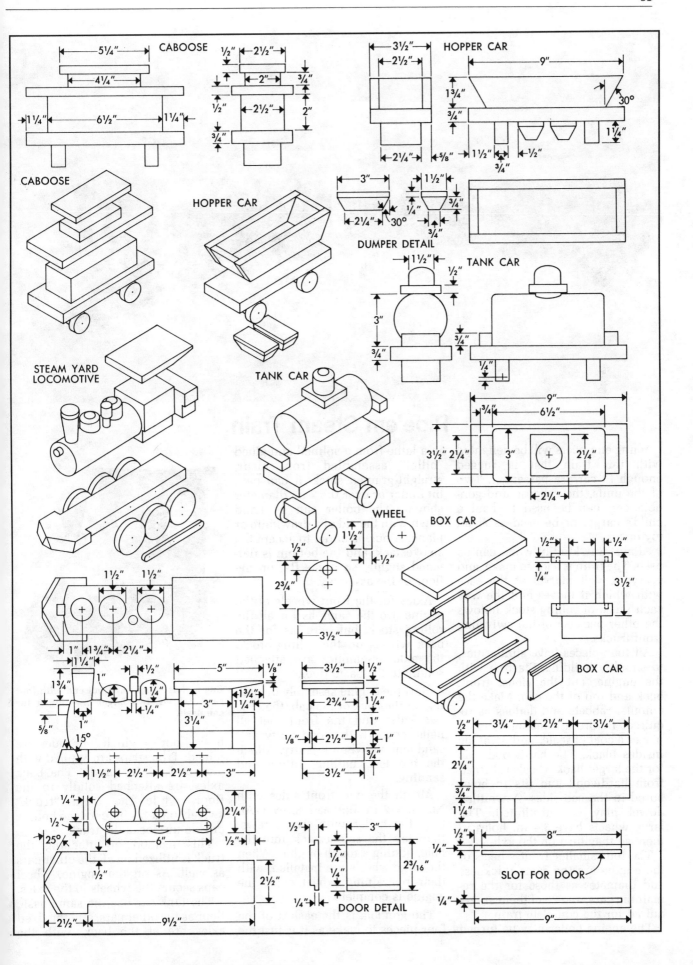

CABOOSE

CABOOSE

HOPPER CAR

HOPPER CAR

DUMPER DETAIL

TANK CAR

TANK CAR

STEAM YARD LOCOMOTIVE

WHEEL

BOX CAR

BOX CAR

DOOR DETAIL

SLOT FOR DOOR

Ride'em Steam Train

Young engineers will be delighted with this train that is rugged enough to carry a passenger. Two of the units, the caboose and gondola car, can be used to haul a child's cargo, or be used as small toy boxes.

Almost any kind of wood can be used. The train is a joy to make, and everyone will marvel at the ease with which it moves and the way each piece of rolling stock follows the other because of the swiveling front trucks.

All four pieces have similarities, to simplify building. Starting with the engine, cut the sides, front, back and top of the cab. Make the cutouts, rabbets and dadoes as required. Before assembing, give all pieces a coat of sealer and paint the insides black. The hardwood axle for the larger back wheels is turned from hardwood and fits in holes bored in the cab sides. A whittled dowel may be substituted. The large wheels have 3/4 in. holes in them so they turn on the axle.

The four smaller front wheels of the engine are the same thickness and diameter as those for the remaining cars, and 28 of them are required for the complete train.

The engine boiler may be turned

in a lathe from a splined and glued "billet" assembled from clear, straight-grained stock. It can be a bit under or over the 7 in. diameter shown. The boiler can be hand hewn with the aid of a drawknife or plane. A hole is bored to accept the smokestack, and the bottom is flattened slightly so it sits flat on the floor of the assembly.

Axles for the front wheels of the engine are the same as for all the rolling stock, but here, as for the back wheels on the rolling stock, the axle assemblies are attached solidly to the basic floor.

Start the engine assembly by nailing on the back of the cab, then the two sides and the front. Set all nails, cover with wood putty and sand smooth when it is dry. Attach the top last, nailing, filling and sanding.

Attach the two front axles with No. 10 x 2 in. flathead screws. Attach the boiler with two screws, then tap the smokestack into the hole, adding a touch of glue. When the large wheels are installed, with their restraining wheel caps, the engine is complete.

The gondola is the easiest of the four pieces to make as it is just the

Engine has "truck" at front end with four small wheels, two larger ones under the cab itself.

basic floor to which four sides are joined. Trim strips are applied with glue and 1/2 in. brads. The back axles are attached solidly to the floor, while the front "truck" swivels on a 1/4 in. carriage bolt. A double nut locks the truck.

This method of attaching the truck is utilized on all the other cars as well. As on the engine, wheel caps secure the wheels to the axles.

The tank car has the same basic floor as the other cars, and the fixed axles are at the back, with the swiveling truck at the front. The tank is made in the same manner as the boiler of the engine.

Tank ends are fashioned from 2 in. pine and made to the same diameter as the tank. A small bevel is cut on the ends of the tank proper, and the two ends, so a V-shape groove is created when the ends are joined to the tank.

Three saddles of 1 in. softwood are cut to the shape indicated. Make the curve to suit your tank, as it may be a bit larger or smaller than the 7 in. suggested for the tank.

Space the saddles on the floor of the car as dimensioned, and fasten them with glue and No. 8 x 2 in. flathead screws, using two for each saddle.

It is easier to enamel all the pieces before assembly. All clearance holes for the screws are drilled first and the car is dry-assembled, then taken apart for painting.

Three colors are used on the tank car: the tank itself is aluminum, the saddles a dark gray and the remainder of the car black. The wheels rotate on well-waxed axles and are held on securely by wheel caps.

Each car has fixed rear truck with four wheels, while front truck pivots on bolt. Note screweyes in trucks.

Cylinder of tank car is painted silver, the saddles are dark gray, while the rest of the car is black.

When the roof is lifted on the caboose it turns out to be a miniature toy box. Use small butt hinges, light chain.

Caboose is painted bright orange, with black wheels, roofs and platforms. Orange also is used inside caboose.

Underside of engine shows how axle for big wheels goes through sides of the cab. Note rabbets.

Every train has a caboose and this one not only is a caboose, but it also serves as a miniature toy box. Construction is simple; the caboose is simply a box with a swing-up lid. The lid is the roof of the caboose plus the cupola and its roof.

To keep weight down, the cupola is assembled from four walls and a one-piece roof.

The roof of the caboose has a

framework to support the two pieces of 1/4 in. plywood or solid stock.

The wheels, floor, roofs and platforms are black; the rest is bright orange, including the inside.

Because it is a pull train, you'll need a stout cord on the engine, at the end of which you can make a loop or attach a length of dowel for a handle.

Between the cars you'll need tow bars, assembled from two "clamps" and a length of dowel. Make the tow bars of hardwood, as they must endure considerable stress and strain.

Screweyes are driven into the front end of each swiveling truck, into the back axle of each car and the back axle of the engine. The ends of the tow bars are fitted over the screweyes, then a 1/4 x 1-1/4 in. carriage bolt and nut is used at each coupling to join the train together.

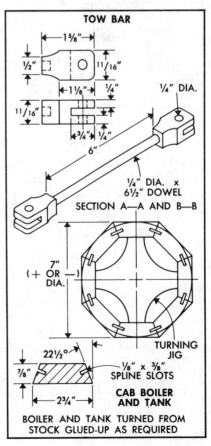

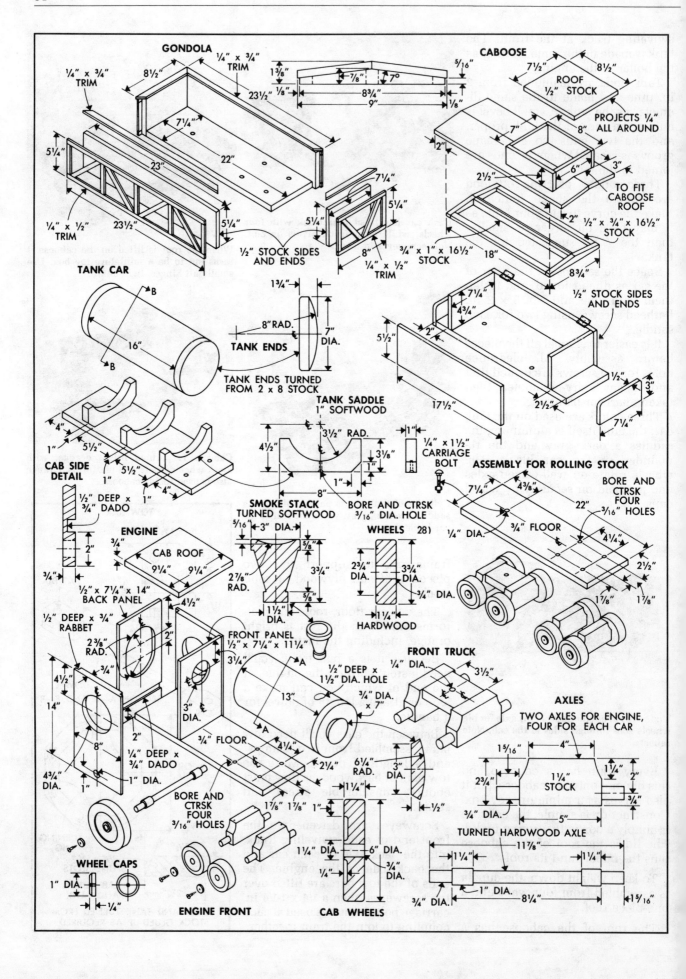

Ride'em Riverboat

A youngster can pretend to be a real riverboat captain with this side-wheeler under his command. It "floats" on two rubber-tired wheels near the front and a rubber-wheeled caster at the stern so no marks are left on the floor.

A stem caster was used for the original but a plate type could be used instead. Be sure the caster is a size that, combined with the wheels, keeps the boat on an even keel.

The hull and cabin get their depth and shape from glued together sections cut from plywood or solid stock as indicated. The hull has a top and bottom, while the cabin has neither. It sits on the hull and the top deck rests on it.

Attach the top and bottom of the hull with glue and screws, after first gluing and screwing the cabin to the top of the hull.

The top deck is machined as detailed in the drawing, then glued and screwed to the top of the cabin.

Note also that two holes in the underside of the top deck near the front, and one at the back, accept dowels that are support columns between the top deck and the top of the hull.

The width and length of the notches in the bottom of the hull may vary a bit from the dimensions

shown, depending on the size of the wheels selected.

The wheelboxes are cut from 1/2 in. plywood and glued and nailed to the sides of the hull. While the wheelhouse on the original is a turning, it can be a rectangle with rounded corners, if you don't have a lathe. A roof should be added, and it overhangs all around. Windows are painted on the front, with a center divider at the very front.

Paint the cabin and the cabin windows before you do the assembly. Any minor flaws that occur during assembly can later be touched up with paint.

The twin smokestacks and the brace between should be solidly glued to the top deck. Bore the 1 in. holes for the stacks all the way through the 3/4 in. thickness of the top deck, so the bottom ends of the stacks rest on the tops of the cabin walls. The reason for the need for strength in the stack assembly is that it is the "handle" by which the young captain will control his craft.

Paint the finished boat in bright colors, then tack a length of rope around the hull near the "waterline" just below the top of the hull. This is the "bumper" to avoid damaging anything with which the riverboat accidentally comes in contact.

Hull is built up with U-shapes for stern, V-shapes for bow cut from 3/4 in. plywood as indicated.

Cabin is assembled in much the same manner as the hull, with built-up U-shapes at each end cut from solid stock.

Rubber-tired wheels are on axles made from 1/2 x 3-1/2 in. cap screws. Wood screws are driven through axles.

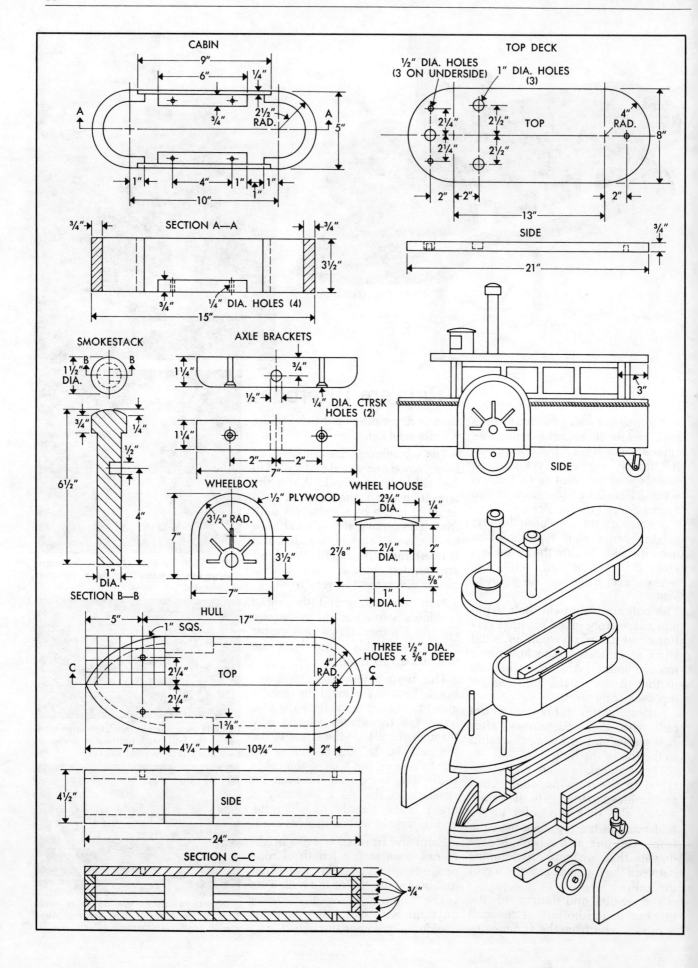

Put a smile on a youngster's face with this "two horsepower" wheelbarrow that rolls on a ball-shape wheel.

Prancing Pony Wheelbarrow

Children love both ponies and wheelbarrows, and this interesting toy combines the two. Easy rolling over most surfaces is assured by using a ball for a wheel. A discarded croquet ball can be utilized, or a ball can be glued up and turned as indicated. Start construction by making a pattern from the squared drawing for the horse outlines. Two pieces of 1/2 in. plywood can be tacked or clamped together and cut at the same time to assure the pony sides being identical. Sand off any saw marks and round all edges. Next, cut to size and sand smooth the two wedges that support the axle. Drill a hole in each wedge to provide slight clearances for the 3/4 in. diameter axles. Glue and nail the wedges to the inner surface of each front hoof of the ponies. Sand smooth the two 18 in. lengths of 1 x 1 in. stock for the handles, and attach the handles to the inside surfaces of the ponies with No. 8 x 1 in. flathead screws driven into the handles through holes drilled in the plywood ponies. Countersink the screws and cover the heads. Cut the floor and backboard of the wheelbarrow from 1/2 in. plywood and attach to one pony only, using 1-1/2 in. finishing nails. Set the nails and cover the heads.

Make the ball-shape wheel next, or drill 3/4 in. blind holes in a croquet ball and insert short lengths of 3/4 in. dowel. Dry fit the second side of the wheelbarrow to the assembly and determine how long the dowel axles must be and cut them to length. Paint the ball and let the paint dry thoroughly. In the meantime, paint all parts of the wheelbarrow inside and out, and paint on the ponies' details.

Assemble the second side to the wheelbarrow, at the same time slipping the axles, which have been wiped with wax, into the holes in the wedges. Use glue and finishing nails to attach the second side. Set the nails, fill the holes with wood putty and when it has set, touch up the enamel job. For an added touch of realism, glue short lengths of unraveled rope to the ponies' necks to simulate manes. Strips of plastic can be glued to the ponies' heads to indicate bridles.

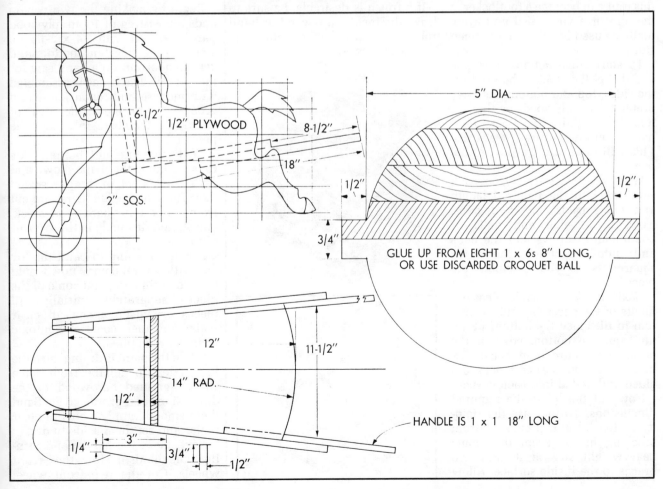

Cedar Toy Chest

Although this toy box could be made of other materials, cedar was chosen for good reason. The span of time a box is used for toys sometimes is relatively short in terms of the lifetime service a well-crafted chest can provide. Made of cedar, this unit can become a footlocker at the end of a youth bed and eventually be used for blanket and linen storage.

To start construction, edge-glue and dowel the stock to be used for the sides, top and bottom. You may prefer to use plywood for the bottom. When gluing the stock, alternate the grain of every other board. This will minimize warping of the panels.

When the pieces are dry, cut each side panel to the required length and miter each end 45 degrees. Now, using glue and nails or countersunk screws join the ends and sides together. Check for squareness as you assemble the pieces.

Next, check the inside measurements of the chest and cut the bottom to fit. Place the bottom 1/2 in. up from the bottom edge of the chest and secure it in place. For more strength, corner blocks are glued and nailed into each corner.

Now cut the lid to the required dimensions. To increase the rigidity of the lid and prevent it from breaking in the event that some heavyweight sits on it, add two braces to the inside surface. Allow enough space at the front and back edge of the lid to permit it to close when the braces are attached.

Position the lid on the chest and screw the hinges in place. Now, invert the chest and attach a caster at each corner.

If a finish is desirable, be sure to leave the inside raw wood or hand rub in an oil which won't inhibit the aromatic fragrance of the natural cedar.

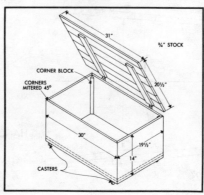

Circus Wagon and Toy Box

Both children and their mothers will like this circus wagon toy box; the kids, because it's a toy they can have fun with and the mothers, because it provides a catch-all for the youngsters' bedroom. Attractive and sturdy enough for even the roughest treatment, the toy box is made of pine with some hardwood used where needed.

Begin by making the two wagon ends, consisting of 1/4 in. plywood panels framed with 3/4 x 2-1/4 in. stock on the sides and bottom and 3/4 in. stock cut on a band saw for the top rail. The frame is assembled with mortise and tenon joints and grooves cut on the inside edges of the frame members to accept the plywood.

Next, the top and bottom side rails are cut to the shape shown and with a 1/4 x 1/4 in. groove sawed their full length. The "bars" are cut from 1/4 x 1 in. hardwood stock, and should fit snugly in the grooves of the rails.

If you are going to paint the toy box with several colors, now would be a good time to paint some of the pieces separately. Initially, all pieces are given a coat of clear sealer and then coats of nontoxic enamel are applied.

While the paint is drying, turn the four axles on a lathe from some straight-grained hardwood to the dimensions and profile given. Sand them smooth, apply a coat of clear sealer and set them aside to dry.

Next, make the handle and turning mechanism for the front wheels. Cut the two front wheel blocks and the handle blocks from hardwood to the shape and dimensions shown. The handle and the front axle spacer also are cut from hardwood, and the six pieces are assembled with glue and screws. When attaching the handle to the handle blocks with the dowel, be careful not to get glue inside the hole in the handle. Glue the dowel only to the blocks so the handle can be moved vertically. Cut the turning plates and the turning-plate stretcher, drill the hole for the carriage bolt and check to see that all the pieces align well and work smoothly.

Cut the rear axle blocks and the floor support cleats. Attach the cleats to the sides with glue and screws, and you're ready to assemble the main body of the wagon. Attach the ends to the sides with glue and screws, but be sure to use finishing washers for a smooth surface. Fit the rear wheel axle blocks to the sides and attach the front wheel block/turning mechanism to the turning stretcher.

Now is the time to decide what kind of wheels to use. The original was made with hardwood wheels turned to the dimensions shown and painted gloss black. If you don't want to go to the trouble of turning wheels, you can purchase ready-made units from a hardware store. Plastic or metal wheels are an alternative, but you will have to make the appropriate changes in the axles that will be used. With any type of wheels, a bolt can be substituted for the wooden axle. After the wheels are on and turning smoothly, cut a piece of 1/4 in. hardboard for the floor and glue it to the cleats.

Finish by sanding and painting as desired and inspect thoroughly for any flaws that might be harmful to children. One last note: if you're going to use wooden wheels and axles, rub some paraffin on the contacting surfaces to reduce friction and assure smooth rotation.

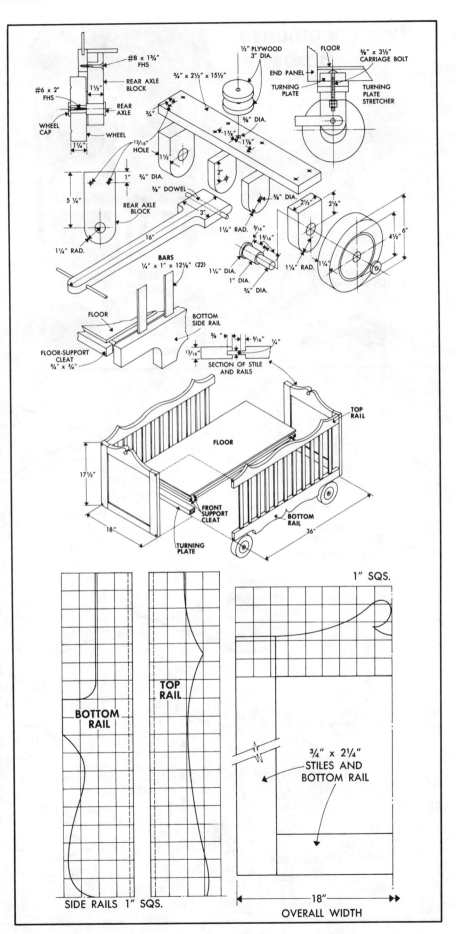

Two Locomotive Toy Boxes

Big enough to play inside and with ample storage room for toys, these locomotives will delight any young Casey Jones. One of the locomotives is for steam fans, the other is a more modern diesel switch engine. Both cabs are identical, but the undercarriage, wheel assemblies and forward part of the units are different.

Assembly has been kept as simple as possible; the only problem might be in making the wheels. They can be rough cut on a bandsaw, then taken to someone who has a lathe and finish cut. Rubber-tired wheels for wagons, tricycles and the like, of approximately this size, also could be used. The railing around the engine of the diesel is made of 6 in. lengths of 1/2 in. dowel, drilled to accept lengths of 1/8 in. dowel.

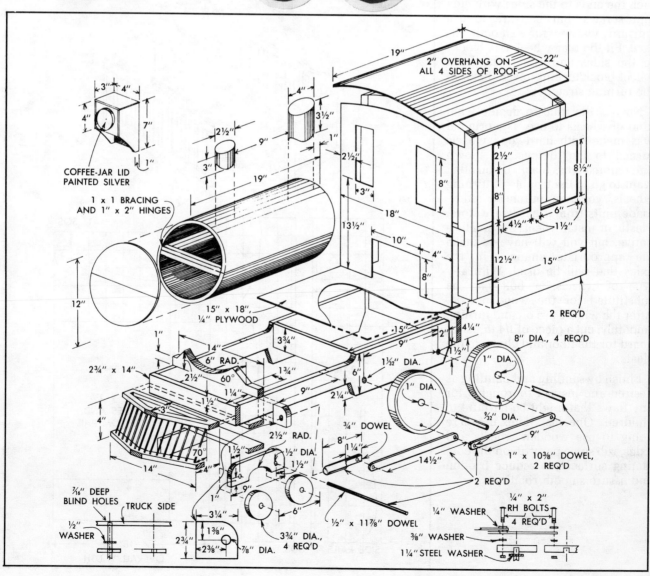

The paint job can be varied to suit the builder's fancy.

The boiler on the steam unit and the engine compartment on the diesel unit are used for toy storage. A framework of 1 x 2s is suggested for the fiberboard drum used for the boiler of the steam locomotive, while the top of the engine compartment on the diesel simply can be fitted with hinges to convert it to a toy box.

All parts of either locomotive should be well sealed to protect against weather before they are painted, as no doubt they will spend some time outdoors. Although not shown, a simple box seat fitted with a cushion could be located on either side of the locomotive cab so that the "engineer" and the "fireman" can each be seated, as in a real locomotive.

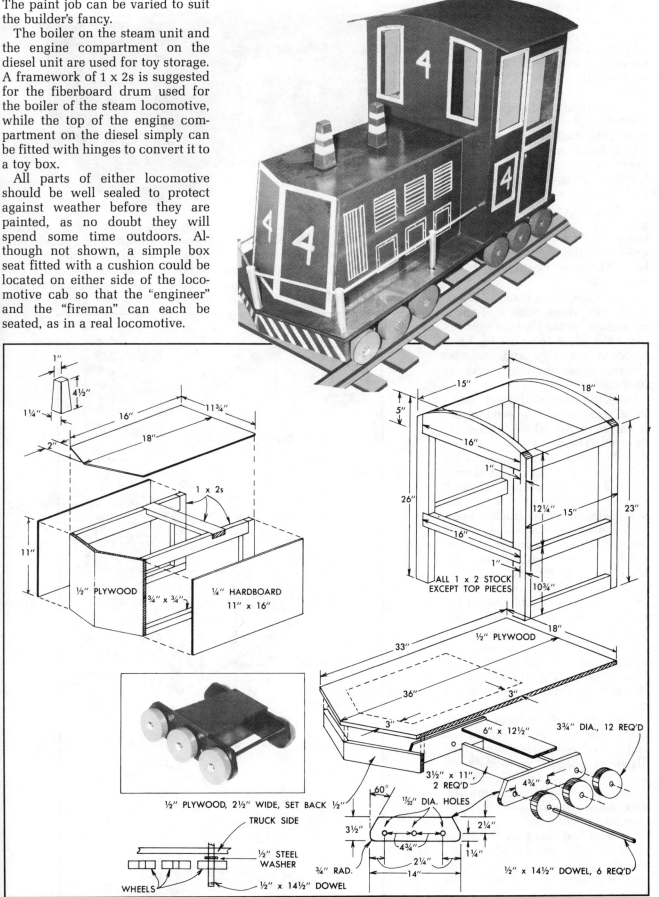

This child size boxcar is really a heavy-duty toy box that can be easily rolled about on eight working wheels. The car is basically a plywood box assembled on a 1/2 in. plywood base. The side and end pieces are cut from 1/2 in. plywood to the dimensions given. The slanted roof frame is assembled from 1 in. stock then covered with 1/4 in. hardboard so that the roof overhangs all around. The roof frame is attached to the sides and ends of the car.

Sliding doors of 1/4 in. plywood give easy access to the roomy interior. The 8-1/2 in. doors slide in grooves in the floor and roof members. The door opening is 16 in. wide.

Each wheel truck consists of two hardwood sides and a T-shape crosspiece assembled as shown. Cut truck sides from 3/4 in. hardwood to 3 x 9 in. and shape as shown. Assemble the trucks as indicated.

Wooden wheels, turned on a lathe, were used in the original, but metal or plastic wheels also could be used. The axles are hardwood dowels coated with paste-wax for non-squeak running. If the wheels you use are different in diameter it may be necessary to re-design the side members of the trucks to provide proper clearance. Also, while both trucks are shown to be fixed solidly, you may wish to pivot one truck so that the car could be steered around corners. To make a pivot, use a 1/4 in. bolt with a flat washer between the frame and truck to assure easier pivoting.

Fixed trucks are attached to the floor of the car with two 1-1/2 in. steel screws. The trucks are attached 6 in. from each end of the car.

The catwalk on the roof is made from four hardwood planks attached to five saddles placed equal distances apart. The saddles are made from softwood, V-notched to fit the roof. When spacing the saddles allow the catwalk a 2 in. overhang at each end.

The end and side trim bracing is made of softwood and adds an air of authenticity. The H-shape on the end measures 4 in. across as shown.

Boxcar Toy Box

The finishing touches for the car are the two vertical access ladders and two roof ladders made to the dimensions shown. For a paint scheme consult your junior railroader or adhere to traditional train colors: red car, black ladders and wheels, brown doors, natural catwalk and red or orange truck sides.

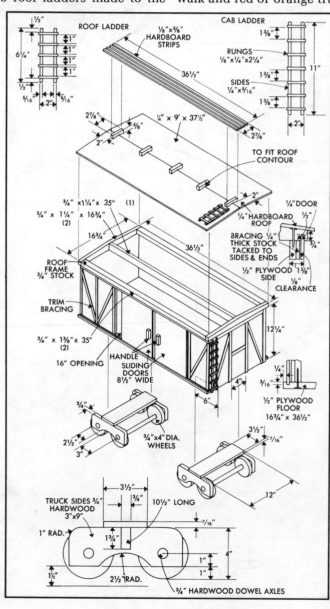

Tank Car Toy Box

Little boys are fascinated by this model railroad tank car that really rolls on its own wheels and doesn't look at all like a container for toys. The youngster can have all kinds of fun wheeling the tank car to where the soldiers and blocks are scattered.

Obtain a cylindrical pasteboard container about 10 in. in diameter from a local merchant for the tank. It will be necessary to cut disks of 3/4 in. plywood to fit in the ends of the container to strengthen it. Cut through the container 4 in. from each end down to the center, then longitudinally to create a "lid" as shown in the drawing. Another 10 in. disk of plywood is cut in half and the halves screwed to the ends of the lid to reinforce it. Use round-head screws to create the appearance of roundhead rivets. Rip strips 1 in. wide from 1 in. solid stock and fit the strips between the half disks of the lid. Attach them to the edges of the lid with roundhead screws. Similar strips are fitted inside the edges of the cutout in the container to reinforce it. A fourth 10 in. disk is cut in half, then sawed to produce half rings 1-1/2 in. wide that are fitted in the ends of the cutout in the container to strengthen the edges. Attach them with roundhead wood screws.

If you cannot obtain a cylindrical container, make the tank from a wooden framework covered with do-it-yourself sheet aluminum that can be purchased at hardware stores. Two disks cut from 3/4 in. plywood, two half-disks and two half rings, as used in the container, are used. The main difference is that the strips on the edges of the

cutout are lengthened and run from end to end of the tank. They are glued and screwed to the end disks. A third stringer is run from end to end, and is positioned at what will be the center of the bottom of the tank. The sheet aluminum is readily wrapped around this framework and is easily cut with tin snips or with heavy-duty scissors. Use roundhead wood screws to simulate roundhead rivets to attach the aluminum, spacing the screws equidistant around the end disks and along the reinforcing stringers. One very real advantage of building the tank with sheet aluminum is that the material already has a shiny metallic finish and needs only a stripe of bright color around each end to look much like a genuine railroad tank car. The pasteboard container first will have to be shellacked, then coated with aluminum paint. The two coatings will be required both to make the tank look realistic and to protect it against wear and tear.

The "frame" under the tank is a rectangle cut from 3/4 in. plywood as indicated in the drawing. The quickest, easiest way to make the cutouts in the frame is with a saber saw. The tank supports are made

next. These can be cut from 1 in. solid stock or 3/4 in. plywood. Solid stock is preferred in this instance as it will provide better holding properties for the screws. Attach the tank supports with glue and screws, then attach the tank with screws driven from inside. If your youngster is liable to climb inside the tank to play, it would be a good idea to provide a third tank support under the center.

The trucks are cut out and assembled as indicated. Wooden wheels, turned on a lathe, were used on the original trucks. The axles are wooden dowels. You may wish to use metal wheels. If wheels of a different diameter are used it may be necessary to redesign the side members of the trucks to provide proper clearance. Also, while both trucks are shown to be fixed solidly to the frame with glue and screws, you may wish to pivot one truck. Then a simple handle could be attached to the truck to enable a youngster to steer. Use a 1/4 in. nut and bolt for the pivot, with a flat washer between the frame and truck.

The ladder is assembled from dowels, the vertical members being 3/8 in., the rungs 1/8 in. Note that the holes for the ladder ends in the frame are angled more than necessary. When the ladder is forced into these holes it is held firmly against the tank and cannot readily be removed.

The tank lid now is hinged to the tank, and a stop-chain is fitted on each side to prevent the lid from falling all the way back and tearing the hinges loose. The "dome" on the tank is made from a cylindrical box, such as used to package salt or oatmeal. Hold the box vertically at the center of the lid and mark around it with a pencil held on a block of wood. Cut along the marked line. The odd-shaped strip

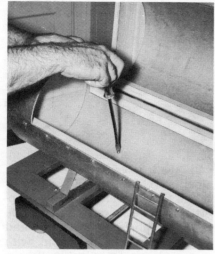

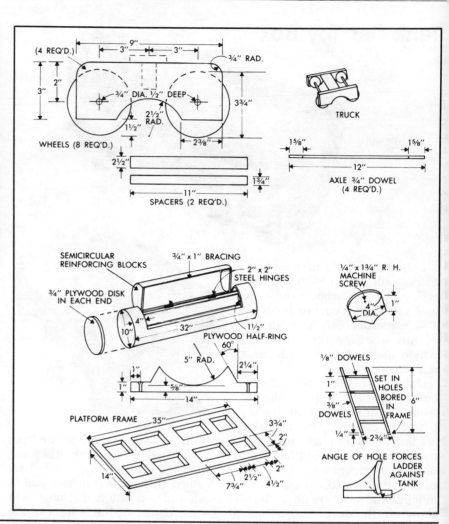

removed now can be used as a pattern and is positioned 1 in. from the top of the box. Mark along the pattern, then cut the dome. Attach it to the center of the top of the lid with a 1/4 in. nut and bolt. Use a flat washer under the head of the bolt and under the nut.

The paint colors used on the tank car can be as varied as you wish, as children love bright colors. The original had a silver tank, the frame was brown, bands on the tank were black, the ladder was bright green, the trucks black and the wheels bright orange.

Caboose Toy Box

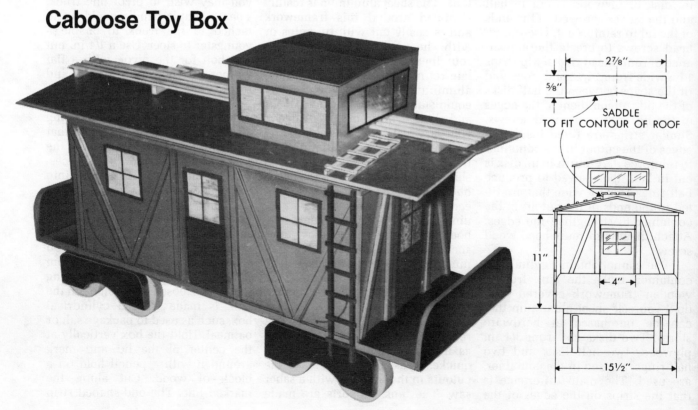

Next to the engine, the car on a train that most interests youngsters is the caboose. It is from here that the conductor directs operations and watches over the long string of freight cars that run from the caboose to the engine. The cupola on top of the caboose is to permit the conductor to see the cars ahead.

This replica of a caboose has a roof that hinges open to permit storage of toys. Hardwood wheels allow the box to be moved around.

Start construction by cutting the ends, sides and floor of the main cab from 1/2 in. plywood. Also cut the guards that fit at the ends of the platforms, and rip 1/2 in. strips from 1/4 in. plywood to create the bracing that is attached to the cab sides. The bracing on the ends of the caboose is cut 3/4 in. wide. Use glue and finishing nails to assemble the caboose and to attach the bracing.

The two trucks are made next. Those on the model shown are fixed, but a pivot could be fitted in one set of trucks to allow the assembly to turn. To steer the caboose, a handle could be fitted to the truck.

Members of the roof framing are ripped from 1 in. stock (3/4 in. net)

and assembled with glue and finishing nails as indicated. Cut the two pieces of hardboard that cover the framework and attach them. Round the edges of the hardboard to eliminate any sharp corners.

Cut the ends and sides of the cupola next. The lower edges of the sides will have to be cut at an angle to match that of the roof of the cab. Check the angle of the roof and match the V-notch of the cupola ends to it.

The cupola is assembled with glue and finishing nails. The hardboard pieces for the roof are cut to size and attached. Attach the cupola to the roof by driving screws up through the hardboard of the roof into the sides and ends of the cupola.

Before putting the catwalks on the roof, paint the roof black or red. When the paint has dried, attach the five saddles, three for the longer catwalk, two for the shorter portion. They are attached by driving screws up through the car's roof. Paint the saddles and the planks for the walks before assembling the walks on the roof. Now glue and nail the planks to the saddles. Also attach the roof planks, which also

should be painted before they are attached.

When attaching the bracing strips on the car's sides and ends, use short brads and glue. Inspect the inside carefully to make sure that none of the brads project through inside. If any do, use two hammers and peen the sharp ends back.

After painting the ends and sides of the caboose and cupola a bright red or yellow, the windows and doors are marked in. Brush or spray the area of the glass with a silver paint, then when it is dry, mask the area and paint in the door and window frame details.

The ladders for the roof and side now are assembled, painted, then fastened in place. The last step is to hinge the roof to the sides of the caboose. Also use a length of chain or a lid support to prevent the top from falling back too far.

The "Grab Bars" at the lower corners of the sides are painted on with black enamel. It is not suggested that they actually be made and attached, as they could be "leg bruisers" for youngsters and would serve no practical purpose. Be sure to use nontoxic paints.

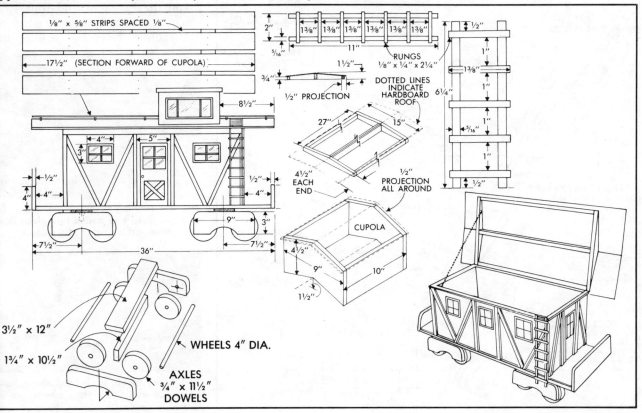

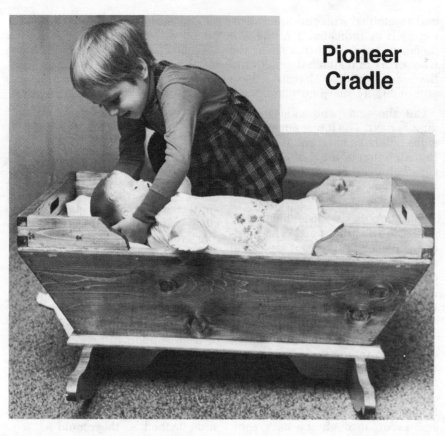

Pioneer Cradle

Destined to become an heirloom itself, this charming cradle is patterned after a century-old home-built model that was found in the attic of a farmhouse.

The cradle shown was built from 1 in. spruce (3/4 in. net), treated with fruitwood stain, then given three coats of clear plastic, satin finish. Pine or any other lumber also could be used.

Start construction by cutting all four edges of the cradle bottom at 62 degrees. Edge-glued stock can be used for the bottom, or you can use a piece of 3/4 in. plywood. With plywood, cut the bottom 1-1/2 in. shorter in length and width, then add 3/4 in. molding, rather than beveling edges as with lumber.

Cut the top and bottom edges of the cradle sides and ends at 69 degrees, the edges of the same pieces at 83 degrees. Assemble the sides and ends with glue and screws in counterbored holes that can be plugged or filled.

Cut and miter the four pieces of trim that fit on the upper edges of the ends and sides. Glue and nail it in place on the upper edges, keeping the outer edges flush with the outer surfaces of the cradle body.

Next step is to cut to size and shape the two end and four side pieces that fit on the upper edges of the cradle at the ends. Use glue and

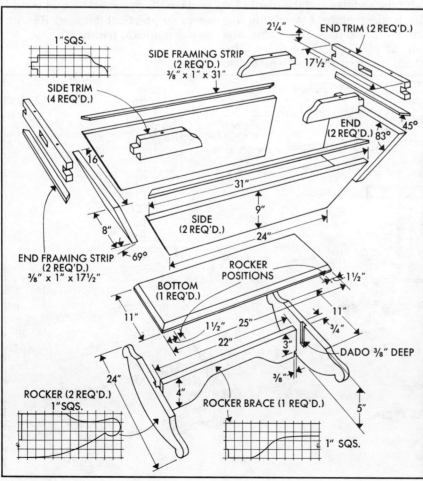

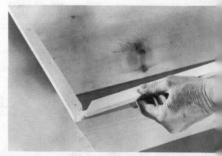

Four top framing strips are mitered at the corners, glued and nailed into place flush with outer surfaces of cradle sides.

End pieces are cut to size and shape, hand holes cut and filed, then pieces are attached to ends with screws.

screws in counterbored holes to attach these six pieces to the cradle. Firm attachment is necessary, as the hand holes in the end pieces are used to lift the cradle.

Cut the rockers to shape, then make the blind mortise at the center of each rocker to accept the tenons on the ends of the stretcher that braces the bottom assembly. Use glue and nails to join the rockers and brace, then attach this assembly to the cradle bottom with screws driven down through the bottom.

Open tenons of side pieces are slipped into end pieces, then side pieces are attached with screws.

Tenons on ends of brace are fitted into blind mortises at the midpoints of the rockers, held with glue and nails.

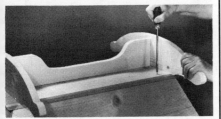

Cradle bottom is screwed to rocker-brace assembly, then bottom is attached to cradle sides and ends with screws.

Finally, turn the cradle body upside down and attach the rocker-bottom assembly to the ends and sides with flathead screws. Countersink the screws well, but they need not be plugged or filled as they will not be seen.

Smooth, sand and fill all surfaces and defects, as well as over countersunk nails and screws that can be seen. Finally, apply your finish.

Swinging Doll Cradle

Almost any little girl would be happy to have this swinging cradle to help put to sleep a cranky doll. Dad or grandfather will appreciate the fact that stock 1 x 4s, 2 x 4s and 1 x 12 shelving, all No. 2 pine, plus some 1/2 and 5/8 in. dowels are all that are required, which makes the project quite inexpensive to build. Additionally you will need to buy, whittle or turn a wooden drawer pull that is used to make the lock for the cradle.

The lock keeps the cradle from swinging, so it can be used for changing diapers and other tasks.

Start construction by assembling the stand that supports the cradle. Cut the end posts, Parts A, after first making a pattern by enlarging the squared half drawing. A notch 3/4 x 1-1/16 in. is cut at the bottom corners to create a tenon.

Next, shape the two "feet." They can be simple strips with the ends rounded or as fancy as you wish. At the center of each foot mark and cut a mortise to accept the tenons on the bottoms of the end posts. Make the mortises a bit undersize, then gradually enlarge them to create a snug fit for the tenons on the posts.

Bore blind holes 5/8 in. in diameter and 9/16 in. deep on the inner face of each post, as shown in the drawing. While the locations of the holes need not be exactly as shown, both holes must be in identical locations to assure the dowel brace being level and on center.

Glue the dowel brace in the blind holes, then position the scrolled stretcher, Part C, centered on top of the feet. Clamp this assembly, square it up and let the glue set at least overnight. Drive small finishing nails through the posts into the dowel brace and the stretcher.

While the glue on the stand is set-ting, cut out and assemble the cradle. Cut the ends, Parts E, from the 1 x 12 shelving. This will require first making a pattern by enlarging the squared drawing. Incidentally, although not previously mentioned, a pattern from the squared drawing also is required for the stretcher, Part C.

Stand for cradle consists of uprights with "feet," scrolled stretcher and dowel brace fitted in holes in uprights.

Side rails, Parts F, of which four are required, are cut from lengths of 5/8 in. dowel. Lay out and drill the seven 3/8 in. holes for the dowel spindles, plus the three in each bottom rail for the bottom dowel supports. Note that the holes for the bottom dowels are at an angle of about 103 degrees in relation to the side spindles. The angle may vary slightly, depending on your assembly, but the spindles should be parallel to the angled edges of the cradle ends.

Bore four blind holes on the inside surface of each end for the rails, and the through hole for the 1/2 x 2-1/2 in. dowel that supports the cradle in the stand. Glue together the side rails, spindles and bottom dowels, then glue this assembly into the two cradle ends.

Make sure the hole in each cradle end is a sliding fit for the dowel, while the hole in each post should be snug. Tap the dowels through the cradle ends into the holes in the posts, with glue in the post holes. Also drive a screw through the side of each post, into the dowel to prevent its turning.

Make the cradle lock as detailed, then drill through one end post and through the cradle end so the lock can be fitted in place. It would not be a bad idea to fasten a light chain to the lock and cradle post to prevent the lock from being mislaid.

When the glue has set, cut a scrap of hardboard, plywood or particle-board for the cradle bottom and drop into place.

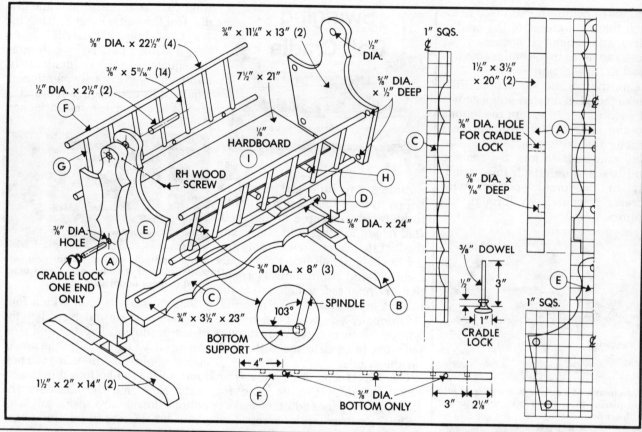

Doll Size Bedroom Furniture

This enchanting bedroom set, proportioned for dolls up to 14 in. tall, consists of four pieces: wardrobe, bed, dressing table and bench seat.

One of the nice things about this project is that it can be made from scraps found in almost any woodworker's shop.

Wardrobe

The basic cabinet and doors are made from 1/2 in. solid stock. You might use softwood and paint it, but hardwood can be used if the piece is to be stained and varnished or lacquered. As an alternative use 1/2 in. hardwood-plywood and cover the edge grain with veneer tape.

The back of the wardrobe, and the backup panels for the door, are cut from 1/8 in. hardboard or plywood.

Start construction with the doors, first making the cutouts, then shaping the outside. Sand both inside and outside edges glass-smooth. Remember that in a scaled down piece of furniture any saw marks or rough spots are even more noticeable than on full size furniture.

Next, cut the 1/8 in. hardboard backup panels 1/4 in. longer and wider than the opening in each door. Cut these panels after you have made the cutouts to allow for any variation in size from the dimensions shown.

This will assure a 1/8 in. overlap on all four sides of the opening. Wrap fabric around the backup panels and glue to the back. You might use scraps for this, and the matching spread on the bed and the pillow on the stool.

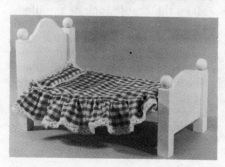

Attach the panels inside the doors with very small roundhead screws or small nails. This will permit easy removal of the panels so the material can be changed at some future date. The panels also should be removed when the wardrobe is painted or stained and finished.

Assemble the rest of the wardrobe with glue and brads, then install the shelves and clothes rod. Paint or finish all parts, then hang the doors with 3/4 x 1 in. butt hinges. A 1/8 x 5/8 in. strip on the right door holds both to the cabinet. Make sure the right door drags slightly to act as a catch.

Dressing Table and Stool

The dressing table is easily assembled from 1/2 or 3/8 in. stock, with a cutout in the front to accept a drawer. The drawer will take a bit of precise fitting, and has sides, front and back made of 1/4 in. stock with the bottom 1/8 in. hardboard. Note that the drawer has a "false front" cut from 1/4 in. stock to lap all around.

The top and bottom drawer guides are strips of 1/4 x 1/4 in. solid stock positioned just above and just below the opening for the drawer.

The mirror supports are 3/8 x 3/4 in. strips 6 in. long. The mirror frame is 1/4 in. plywood or solid stock. The dresser shown has a "mirror" of aluminum foil glued to the frame. A scrap of lightweight mirror could be cut to size and recessed into the frame for a more realistic appearance.

The bench seat for the dressing table is a scaled down version of the table and should offer no difficulties in assembling. One change you might want to make is to hinge the top of the seat and create a small storage space under it. This would require installing a bottom of 1/8 in. hardboard also. The bottom could be fitted in grooves cut on the inner surfaces of the four sides, or small cleats could be glued and bradded inside to support it.

Bed

About the only items you won't have in the scrap box for making the bed are the round balls on the tops of the corner posts. These were purchased at a craft shop and come in a variety of sizes. If you are a lathe buff, the spheres could be easily turned.

Attach the balls with a small dowel; the wooden beads you buy in a hobby shop will already have holes in them and you simply glue a dowel in the hole, and in a hole bored in the top of each bedpost.

A mattress can be fashioned from a piece of scrap foam rubber or urethane fitted in a cloth sleeve made to fit it. Pillows could be made the same way.

No instructions are given for the spread or pillow on the bed or the pillow on the stool. That is left to the discretion of the builder.

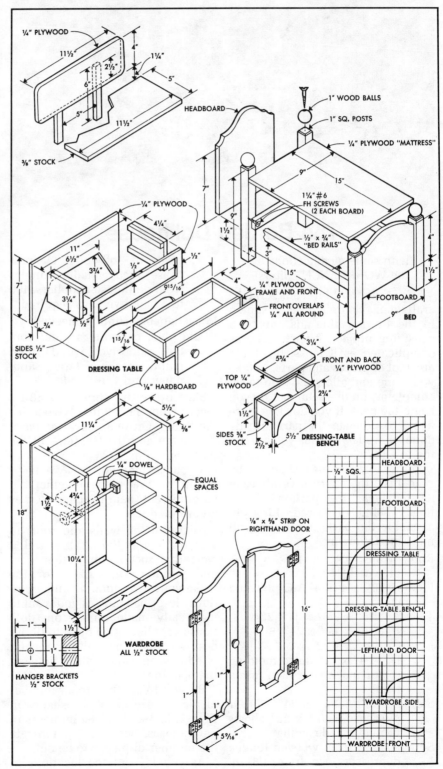

The Borden Dollhouse

(with some modifications by the WORKBENCH editors)

For the "build-it-from-scratch" craftsman this dollhouse as shown in the Borden glue ads can be a satisfying project. It isn't really as complicated as it looks, but there are a lot of pieces and parts, so take your time and allow the glue to set completely on one setup before you begin the next. If you don't, you are liable to damage the part already done, as well as the one you are trying to add.

Rather than having just one Materials List, there are several, each located near the portion of the house being discussed. First, to assemble the basic house you will need the following:

Roof, Walls, 1/4" x 4' x 8' A-C plywood (1)

Floors, 3/8" x 4' x 4' A-C plywood (1)

Trim A, 1/16" x 3/8" x 24" (22)
B, 3/16" x 1/4" x 24" (6)
C, 1/16" x 1-1/2" x 24" (2)
D, 1-1/4" x 12" fluted molding (1) (or make your own fascia trim)

Siding, 1/16" x 1/2" x 24" (70) Or purchase 3-1/2" x 22" sheets of ready made siding

Shingles, cut from wooden tongue depressors, or from 1/8 in. strips of softwood. Or purchase ready made shingles from dollhouse suppliers, 100 to a bag, two bags required.

Miscellaneous supplies needed:

White glue, carpenter's glue, contact adhesive, wood filler, paint, masking tape, sandpaper and 1 in. brads.

Start by cutting three 13 x 48 in. pieces from the 3/8 in. plywood for the floors. On one, mark the basic floor plan and the locations of the partitions, Fig. 1. When you have one sheet marked, tack nail or clamp the three pieces together and carefully cut them to shape so they all are identical.

Next, cut the walls and roofs to size and shape, Figs. 2, 3, 4 and 5. Note that the openings for doors and windows are sized for the make-your-own doors and windows described later. If you want to use ready made units from dollhouse suppliers, size them to fit. It's best to actually have the doors and windows on hand before you cut the openings.

Be sure to cut the proper number of pieces of each of the shapes in Figs. 2, 3, 4 and 5. The numbers in parentheses, such as (2), indicate the number of pieces to be cut.

As you lay out the locations of window and door openings also mark the positions of the second floor and attic floor. Make sure the marks are on the inside surfaces of the various pieces. The "good" or "A" side of the plywood should be on the inside, while the "C" or "poor" side is on the outside where it will be covered by the siding.

Also, when making wall and roof pieces that are in pairs, as "D" in Fig. 3 and "Z" in Fig. 5, clamp the plywood with the "A" sides together. Roof pieces also have the "A" side inward (down) because the roof shingles will cover the rougher "C" side of the plywood.

After all the pieces have been cut to size and shape, check all edges for voids and all surface areas for dents or scratches. Use wood filler and a putty knife to fill voids and imperfections, let dry, then sand smooth.

Fast-tack carpenter's glue and 1 in. brads are used for the assembly of the dollhouse. After the brads are driven, immediately wipe off any excess glue with a damp cloth. If you miss any of the glue, it can be scraped off after it dries with a sharp wood chisel. Once you have glued up an assembly, let it stand for at least 12 hours to make sure the glue has set completely.

If you have bar clamps they certainly would be a help in making the dollhouse, but if you don't have clamps the glue and brads will hold the pieces in place until the glue sets. One help is to apply the carpenter's glue, then expose it to the air for about 30 seconds. It will set up slightly for a faster "grab" and the pieces being joined will not move easily.

Carefully examine Fig. 6 to see how the various components are joined in the assembly. Start by attaching wall sections "B" to the first floor, then add front wall "A" and sections "C" and "D." Glue and brad interior walls "E" to the first floor and to the edges of walls "B."

Next, glue and brad interior walls "F" on top of the second floor, where you marked the locations. Clamp blocks on one or both sides of the walls to keep them square with the floor and let the glue set completely. When the glue has set, slip the floor/walls assembly into

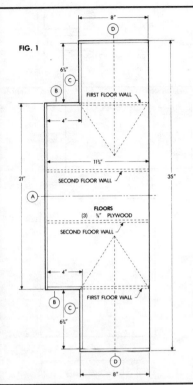

FIG. 1

the house on top of the first floor interior walls. Mark along the top and bottom of the floor and on each side of the walls, on the outside walls of the house, then remove the assembly. Apply a thin line of glue along between the marks, then install the floor/walls assembly and brad it where possible.

As indicated at the top of Fig. 4, gluing and bradding a small crown or cove molding on the walls will provide additional support and nailing surfaces for the floors.

Insert the attic floor, mark the edges on the walls, remove and apply glue, then fit the floor in place. Let the basic house assembly set at least 12 hours after the last glue is applied to make sure the structure is solid.

Attach the roof beginning with center sections "Y." To assure a rigid assembly during construction, make a temporary back gable "X" the same size and shape as the upper, angled portion of front wall "A." Glue and brad the two "Y" roof pieces to the top of wall "A" and clamp or loosely brad the temporary gable at the other ends of the "Y" roof members.

Position each of the four roof pieces "Z" against the "Y" roof members and mark along the underside on the "Y" pieces. Posi-

tion one piece at a time and remove it and set it aside. Now, cut and attach the four 1/8 x 1/8 x 4 in. support strips with glue, under the lines made to mark the locations of the "Z" pieces. At this point, let the house set for 12 hours to allow the glue to set up completely.

At the next work session, use glue and brads to attach roof sections "Z." The basic house is finished and ready for the "finishing touches." If you don't want to apply siding, use filler to fill in any defects, let it dry, then sand smooth. Paint a suitable color.

You can buy ready-made siding in panels, or cut your own from 1/16 x 1/2 x 24 in. strips of balsa or other wood. Start at the bottoms of the walls and overlap each preceding strip by about 1/8 in.

Roof shingles can be purchased, or you can cut 1/4 x 3/4 in. pieces from 1/8 in. lattice stock. If trim on the house is to be a contrasting color, paint it before attaching it to the already painted house. The trim strips can be bradded on over the siding, but a more professional look will be achieved by installing the trim strips first, then prepainting

the siding, cutting it to butt against the trim, then touching up the paint where necessary with a tiny brush. The molding strips "A" are indicated in Fig. 7 as to location, including those on each side of the ridge of the roof. The latter is attached over the shingles. When all this work is done, remove the temporary gable "X."

Brackets that fit against the fascia and up against the underside of the roof overhang are 1/2 in. slices cut from small molding, with the tops beveled to fit against the roof.

While only one bay window is shown on the house, Fig. 8, you might want two, one for each end. In this case, double the number of pieces in the Materials List.

Bay Window Materials List
a, 1-15/16" x 5-1/4" clear plastic (3)
b, c, d, e and f are dimensioned on
    drawing, with number required
g, 1/8" x 1/4" x 1-7/16" (6)
h, 1/8" x 1/4" x 5-1/4" (6)
i, 1/8" x 1/8" x 1-7/16" (3)
j, 1/8" x 1/8" x 3/4" (6)

The edges of parts "e" and "f" are beveled with sandpaper, as are the edges of the six "h" strips that meet to form the bay and contact the

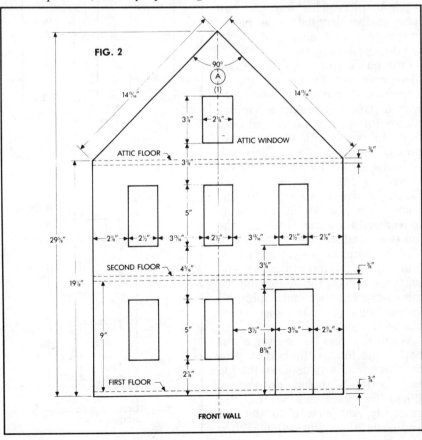

FIG. 2

wall. If any joints do not meet exactly, fill voids with filler, let it dry and sand smooth. The clear plastic is glued to the backs of the three windows in the bay.

There are 12 "regular" windows and one for the attic. All windows have a pair of shutters, but the attic window does not have the detailed cornice above as do the other windows. Note that the trim for the windows goes both inside and outside of the window openings.

Materials List for Windows and Shutters

a, 1/8″ x 1/2″ x 4″ (12)
b, 3/8″ x 3/8″ x 3-1/2″ (12)
c, 1/4″ x 1/4″ x 3-1/4″ (48)
d, 1/8″ x 1/8″ x 2-7/8″ (24)
e, 1/8″ x 3/8″ x 4-3/4″ (48)
f, 1/8″ x 1/8″ x 2-1/16″ (12)
g, 1/16″ x 3/16″ x 1-1/4″ (50)
h, 1/16″ x 3/16″ x 4-1/4″ (48)
i, 1/16″ x 1-1/4″ x 4-5/8″ (24)
j, 1/8″ x 3/8″ x 3-3/8″ (4)
k, 1/8″ x 3/8″ x 3-5/8″ (4)
l, 1/16″ x 3/16″ x 3″ (4)
m, 1/16″ x 1-1/4″ x 3-3/8″ (2)

After cutting the various pieces to size, lightly mark them with a pencil so you can tell which is the a, b, c, etc., then place them in separate piles. This way you can more easily select the proper pieces to position and glue around the window openings.

One quick and accurate method of assembling the windows is to use a softwood board covered with waxed paper. Position the various pieces for each window and hold them in place with pins or push pins while the glue sets. There will be some glue squeeze-out, but the waxed paper will prevent the assembly from sticking to the board, and excess glue can be removed with a razor knife and the joints sanded smooth.

Make "sandwiches" of parts b, c, b and d for the top of the bay, and parts d and b for the bottom, gluing the pieces together and wiping off excess glue after the pieces are clamped together.

When the glue has set for a few hours (the longer the better), glue the three windows between the top and bottom, angled as shown. When the glue has set on this assembly, add parts "e" for the roof and parts "f" for the bottom. When the glue has set for at least 12 hours, attach the bay window to the opening on the house.

The regular windows, attic window and the shutters are assembled in much the same fashion as the individual windows for the bay, using a board covered with waxed paper. When all the frames are assembled and the glue has set, install them inside and outside the window openings as indicated. Clear plastic is indicated for the windows and will create a more authentic appearance, but can be eliminated if you wish.

The very attractive door for the dollhouse, Fig. 9, is assembled from a number of pieces, as is the facade that fits along both sides and over the top.

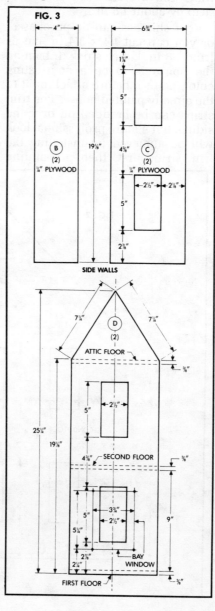

Materials List for Door

a, 1/8″ x 5/8″ x 4-3/8″ (2)
b, 1/2″ x 9/16″ x 13/16″ (2)
c, 1/8″ x 3/4″ x 4-5/8″ (1)
d, 1/2″ x 9/16″ x 1-1/4″ (2)
e, 1/8″ x 1/2″ x 5-9/16″ (2)
f, 1/4″ x 5/8″ x 3/4″ (2)
g, 1/8″ x 3/8″ x 3-1/8″ (1)
h, 1/4″ x 1″ x 1-15/16″ (2)
hh, 1/4″ x 1″ x 1-1/2″ (2)
i, 1/4″ x 1″ x 1-3/16″ (2)
j, 1/4″ x 1″ x 1-3/8″ (2)
k, 1/8″ x 3/16″ x 2-15/16″ (1)
l, 1/8″ x 1/2″ x 2-15/16″ (1)
m, 1/8″ x 3/16″ x 8-5/8″ (2)
n, 3/32″ x 1/2″ x 1-13/16″ (4)
o, 3/32″ x 1/2″ x 3/4″ (1)
p, 3/32″ x 1/2″ x 2″ (2)
q, 3/32″ x 1/2″ x 6-7/8″ (2)
r, 1/8″ x 3/8″ x 2-15/16″ (1)
s, 1/4″ x 2-7/8″ x 6-7/8″ (1)

Use the board with waxed paper method as for the windows and assemble the facade and door. If you want the door to open, build the door separate from the facade and hinge it to the facade. It will have to swing inward, of course, as

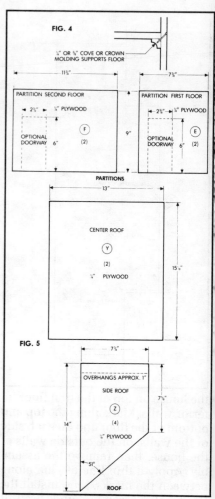

the facade would prevent it opening out. Exterior doors on full size houses almost always open inward. Storm sash and screen doors open outward.

While assembling the bay window, the regular windows and the door and facade, paint them before attaching them to the house if they are to be a different color than the house. Don't, of course, paint the interior window trim.

The basic dollhouse now is complete and ready for interior decorating and furnishing. As carpenter and contractor your job is finished and the rest is up to the new owner.

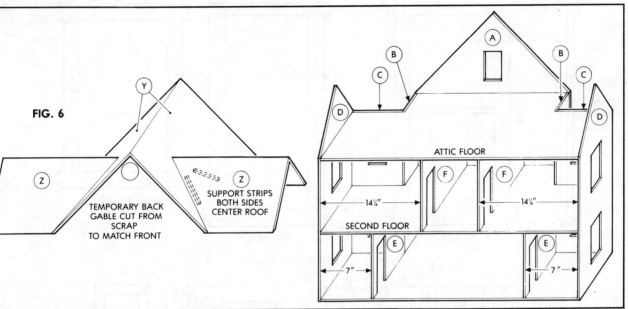

FIG. 6

TEMPORARY BACK GABLE CUT FROM SCRAP TO MATCH FRONT

SUPPORT STRIPS BOTH SIDES CENTER ROOF

ATTIC FLOOR

14¼" 14¼"

SECOND FLOOR

7" 7"

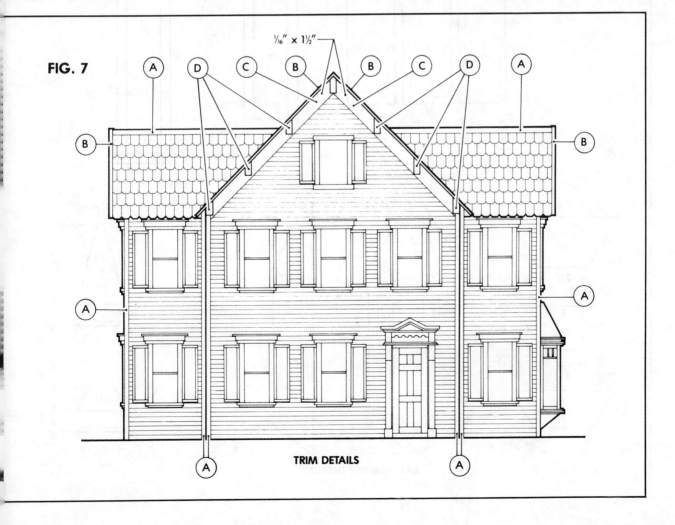

FIG. 7

1/16" x 1½"

TRIM DETAILS

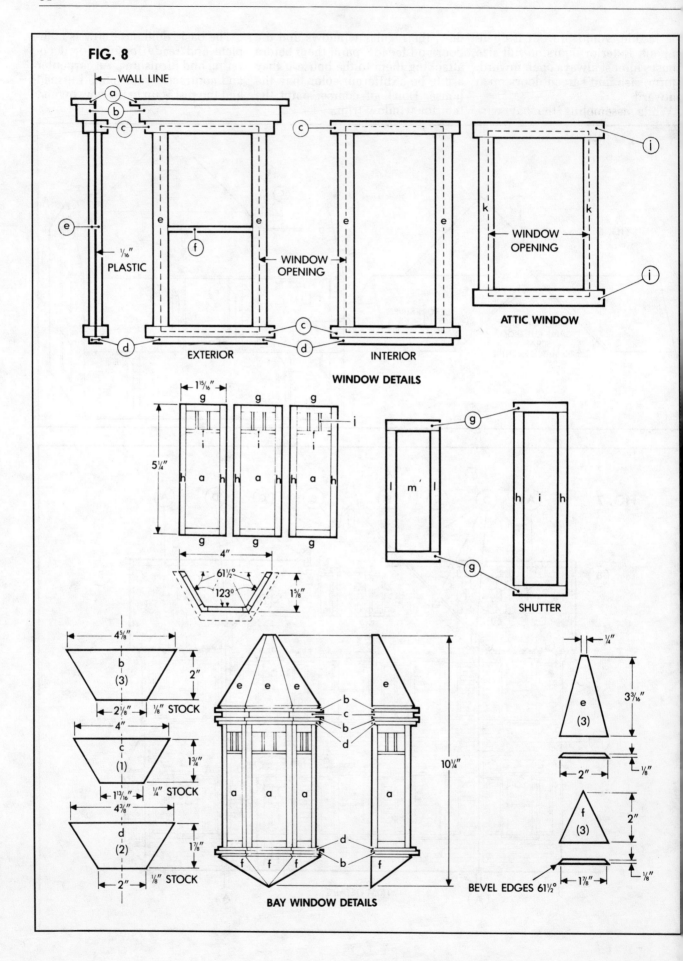

FIG. 8

WALL LINE

PLASTIC
1/16"

EXTERIOR

WINDOW OPENING

INTERIOR

ATTIC WINDOW

WINDOW OPENING

WINDOW DETAILS

1 15/16"

5 1/4"

4"

61 1/2°

123°

1 5/8"

SHUTTER

4 5/8"

b (3)

2"

2 1/8"   1/8" STOCK

4"

c (1)

1 3/4"

1 13/16"   1/4" STOCK

4 3/8"

d (2)

1 7/8"

2"   1/8" STOCK

BAY WINDOW DETAILS

10 1/4"

1/4"

e (3)

3 3/16"

2"

1/8"

f (3)

2"

1/8"

BEVEL EDGES 61 1/2°

1 7/8"

FIG. 9

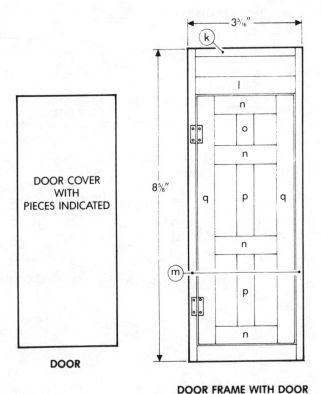

DOOR FACADE   SECTION THROUGH DOOR

65° 65°

70° 83½°   83½° 70°

9⁵/₃₂″

3⅛″

FRAME → | ← FACADE

DOOR COVER
WITH
PIECES INDICATED

DOOR

3⁵/₁₆″

8⅝″

DOOR FRAME WITH DOOR

Toddler Sled

Basically a hand-tool project, this wooden sled is patterned after those made many years ago. It's very practical for toddlers, and the only change that might be required would be the addition of steel strips on the runners if you live in an area of light snowfall.

The back and sides keep the toddler snuggly in place when someone takes the youngster for a ride. An ordinary piece of rope can be used for pulling.

Stock for the sled should be a tough, durable wood such as oak, hickory or ash in at least 1/2 in. net thickness.

The first step is to enlarge the squared drawings and make patterns for the back, sides and runners, and for the front of the sled. Cut all pieces to size and shape. The curves can be cut easily with a coping or jig saw, and by clamping the two sides and two runners together, you will be sure of exact pairs.

Thoroughly sand each piece, then apply several coats of exterior spar or urethane varnish before you assemble the sled. Assemble the sled with brass screws, rather than steel, to avoid rusting. For an added touch, apply decorative decals and coat with varnish. You may not be able to find a brass screweye, so use a zinc or cadmium-plated one to which to tie the tow rope.

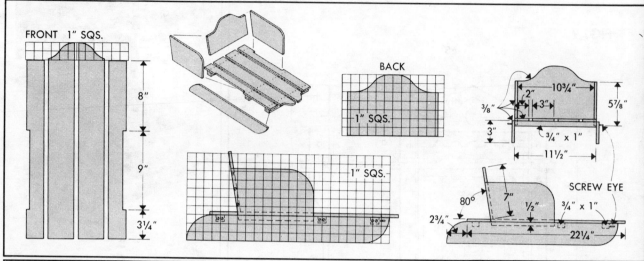

FRONT 1" SQS.

8"

9"

3¼"

BACK

1" SQS.

1" SQS.

1" SQS.

10¾"

2"

3"

⅜"

5⅞"

3"

¾" x 1"

11½"

SCREW EYE

80°

7"

½"

¾" x 1"

2¾"

22¼"

Children's Surrey Sled

Pulled by hand or towed behind a garden tractor or a snowmobile, this lightweight sleigh will give youngsters a thrilling ride.

The squared drawing illustrates the compact dimensions on an 18 x 72 in. marine plywood chassis. Using a full 8 ft. length of plywood will permit adding a third seat. The side members are 1 in. pine or redwood (3/4 in. net) for lightness and are assembled with waterproof glue and corrugated fasteners. Glue and screws are used to fasten these assemblies to the plywood floor.

Runners are conventional snow skis, available at sport shops, or you can make your own from 3/8 x 4 in. hickory. Soak or steam the ends for bending, then place them in a form until the wood sets. Trim the blanks to shape after bending. Auto leaf springs, heated and bent to shape, can be used in place of the flat-steel suspensions.

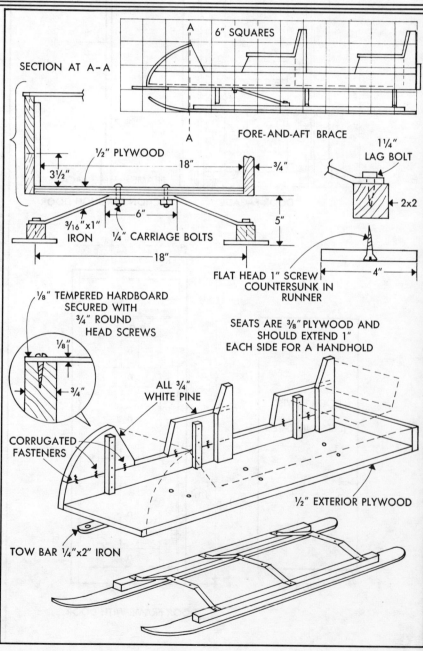

6" SQUARES

SECTION AT A-A

A

A

FORE-AND-AFT BRACE

1¼"
LAG BOLT

½" PLYWOOD

18"

¾"

3½"

2x2

2"

³⁄₁₆" x1"
IRON

6"

¼" CARRIAGE BOLTS

5"

18"

FLAT HEAD 1" SCREW
COUNTERSUNK IN
RUNNER

4"

⅛" TEMPERED HARDBOARD
SECURED WITH
¾" ROUND
HEAD SCREWS

⅛"

¾"

SEATS ARE ⅜" PLYWOOD AND
SHOULD EXTEND 1"
EACH SIDE FOR A HANDHOLD

ALL ¾"
WHITE PINE

CORRUGATED
FASTENERS

½" EXTERIOR PLYWOOD

TOW BAR ¼"x2" IRON